B

with *Emily Black*

The Artist Disciple

A guidebook for transforming the world through your art

Copyright © 2013 by Brydon Brett

All rights reserved. Except as permitted under the U.S. Copyright Act of 1976, no part of this publication may be reproduced, distributed, or transmitted in any form or by any means without the prior written permission of the author.

This is not an official publication of The Church of Jesus Christ of Latter-day Saints. The opinions and views expressed herein belong solely to the author. Permission for use of sources, graphics, and photos is solely the responsibility of the author.

All *Artist-Disciple Insights,* personal stories and/or quotations from Artist-Disciples are used with written consent.

The Artist-Disciple, LLC.
119 Westwood Dr.
Branson, MO 65616
Visit our Web site at www.theartistdisciple.com

First Edition: August 2013

Cover design by Gavin Boothe
Illustrations by Saul Hansen
Formatting by Polgarus Studio

Contents

Acknowledgments 1

Introduction 3

Section I:
Vision

Lesson 1

    The Vision of Artist-Discipleship 9

Lesson 2

    The Power 23

Lesson 3

    The Problem 45

Section II:
Forming the Upstream

Lesson 4

    The Foundation 65

Lesson 5

    The Lodestar 89

Lesson 6

    The X Factor 111

Lesson 7

    Revelation 133

Section III:
Transformational Creation

Lesson 8

    Transformational Creation 161

Lesson 9

    Excellence 181

Lesson 10

    The Secret Ingredients 207

Section IV:
Influence

Lesson 11

    Influence 227

Lesson 12

    Legacy 245

Thanks…

To my Heavenly Father, my Savior Jesus Christ, and the Holy Ghost for the power, mercy and inspiration I've been given for this project. Anything good that comes out of this book will be because of grace.

To my mom and dad, as well as my brother and sister, Briahna and Garon. I never would have or could have finished this project without your strength, love and support. Someday we'll write our own book about how we've stuck together and made it work as a show-biz family.

To Emily Black, whose miraculous co-writing help and exceptional leadership really made this project possible. Also, to Melanee Green Evans, Saul Hansen, Dele Opeifa, Angela Linton, Rachel Andersen, Sean Higgins, Gavin Boothe and Debbie Hansen—*The TAD Dream Team* that the Lord brought together to get this book to the finish line. I learned so much about team and trust through this process. You all have been ministering angels.

To everyone in the TAD Community (particularly the initial TAD 101 Course graduates). Your participation, contribution and feedback have been absolutely invaluable. There is no way this project would have gotten off the ground without you.

To my bandmates, Aaron Ellsworth and my brother Garon, for being patient and supportive as I have had to take the necessary time to fulfill this part of my personal mission. What we do together with our music will hopefully be an embodiment of the principles contained in this book.

To Randal Wright, Kordell Norton, Jeff Benedict and others in the writing and speaking world who have mentored me, inspired me and given me professional advice.

To *The Bretts Power Team*—Joshua Hall, Rebecca Murphy, Casey Hall, Lynn Henry and Kenneth Reitmeier—for always being encouraging and supportive and for helping us maintain the business-side of what we do so that we and I could focus on creative projects like this.

To all of my friends, fans, acquaintances, influences, mentors, coaches and family members. Nothing great is ever accomplished alone and I am extremely grateful for the help I have received upward, downward, and sideways from truly too many people to mention.

This book, and anything that stems from it is dedicated "as unto the Lord" to the building up of the Kingdom of God and the hastening of the work of salvation. May it ignite personal vision, power and inspiration in the lives of individuals and be an irresistible force for goodness, transformation and action in the lives of families, communities and nations throughout the world.

Introduction

08 May, 2008

"It's time to call your coach." For the first twenty-four years of my life, basketball was basically it. Other than the gospel, my family and school, it was the thing I dedicated all of my time, talents and energy to. I dreamed of playing professional basketball. I watched every game, knew every stat, read every magazine. I even slept with my basketball and gave my different basketballs names like Roxanne, Trenyce and other embarrassing appellations. The point is that, growing up, Brydon Brett and basketball were synonymous. After serving my mission in Portland, OR, I came home and experienced a little loss of fire for basketball, but still had every intention of pursuing a semi-professional career or at least a career in coaching. Basketball was still the direction I was going.

In the spring of 2008 I was coming off a challenging but rewarding freshman season at Southern Virginia University and was slated for a starting position the next year. The program was headed in the right direction—great recruiting class, new coach and a strong cast of returning players. We were expected to do great things. Everything in my past and in my DNA indicated that I should pursue basketball. So, imagine my surprise when my course was derailed by the still, small, but persistent, "It's time to call your coach." Now, this message didn't come completely out of the blue. I had been deliberating for months about life without basketball, but had finally arrived at that proverbial fork in the road where you have to follow what you've received or you won't receive anymore. So, I called my coach. I told him regretfully that I had to quit the team, give up my athletic scholarship and pursue…well I didn't entirely know what. I hung up the phone and leaned back in my chair.

The next 45 minutes was one of those rare and to-be-cherished crystalizing experiences where much of my life was laid out before me and my immediate course was made clear. At that point I had been performing with my family in Branson, MO for about 9 or 10 years, but I'd never opened my eyes to the opportunity that was in front of me. Basketball was always where my heart was and I had no intention of pursuing a career in music. But now, after serving a mission and going away to college, I was beginning to see Branson, performing with my family, and pursuing a career in music with a more mature perspective. I caught a glimpse of the power and influence I could have and the good I could do for the Kingdom through music. I decided to be an artist.

At that moment I also felt the spark for *The Artist-Disciple* project. I saw the chance to help mobilize other artists to make a positive difference in the world as well. I began researching and preparing. Line upon line, conversation upon conversation, and experience upon experience, the purpose and content of the project were revealed and discovered.

29 Dec. 2010

"It's time to write." It had been about 2 ½ years since my decision to be an artist. I had been working in the background on *The Artist-Disciple* during that time and was relatively comfortable with the pace the project was keeping. On this particular morning though, these words came forcefully to my mind: "It's time to write." My perfectionist-self argued, "But I'm not ready. No one's going to listen to a 26 year-old boy who only just recently became serious about music. I need many more years of musical and creative experience and a long list of credentials before anyone will listen to what I have to say." Still, I felt compelled to do it, to finish something, to really get the process started. So, despite not feeling prepared, I moved forward, trusting that the Lord would guide me in my weakness and He did.

After beginning to write the book in earnest, one of the pivotal steps I was inspired to take was to conduct a course with real people to see how the material in the book would connect with an audience. Thus the TAD 101 Course was born. Some 30 of us had a magical twelve-week experience learning and growing together in the summer and fall of 2011. That initial group of 30 has now developed into a growing community of Artist-Disciples from all over the world, and we stay in frequent contact to strengthen and support each other. Through my experience with the TAD Community I learned the clear and present need for the material in this book.

Many other inspired steps and miracles followed to allow the book and project to get its footing. Most recently I was led to as fine a group of people as I know who I have dubbed the *TAD Dream Team*. This incredible team of editors, managers, marketers and designers helped me, with my busy performing schedule, to get the TAD project officially launched. I'd like to give special thanks and recognition to the amazing Emily Black, who the Lord brought to TAD at a critical time to help co-write the book and guide the project to completion, which leads us to today.

01 August, 2013

"It's time to mobilize." These words capture the overall feeling that is burning in my heart right now. The purpose of *The Artist-Disciple* project is to encourage, educate, inspire, and mobilize the LDS creative community. Its ultimate goal is to empower you to use your creative gifts to fulfill your personal mission, build up the Kingdom of God, and help prepare the earth for the Second Coming. Many Artist-Disciples are already working effectively to transform the world and I believe it is time for all of us to take our place on the team and fulfill our divine missions. I know that the principles in this book and the inspiration in *The Artist-Disciple* project as a whole are needed today and can make a difference in your life immediately.

Just a few words about the book itself. It is broken down into four different sections: Vision, Forming the Upstream, Transformational Creation and Influence. Hopefully this convention gives context to the twelve chapters as you read them. You'll also enjoy the *Artist-Disciple Insights* segments, which precede each chapter with different stories and/or insights from Artist-Disciples just like you. The *Questions and Action Items* box at the end of each chapter is a good checkpoint for you to pause and reflect on the content of the book so far. I would encourage you to have a study journal and pen close by to capture insights and inspiration as the layout of the content is designed to prompt personal exploration and personal revelation. Lastly, pay attention to the diagrams and illustrations, which are also designed to provoke thought and further exploration. When you are ready to enhance your study and connect with other Artist-Disciples, just go to www.theartistdisciple.com. There you will find opportunities to learn more, network, and go to the next level as an Artist-Disciple by participating in the *TAD 101 Course* yourself.

The path of the artist is a treacherous road with many pitfalls. In my strivings to become a true Artist-Disciple I have missed the mark many times and will probably continue to do so. You will too. We are imperfect fellow travelers exploring this path together. I make no claim to be an expert or the perfect practitioner of the principles espoused in this book. I am simply striving to follow the directions I have received. I am grateful for those messages and impressions that have led me to this point and I am excited to finally present *The Artist-Disciple* to the world. I hope you find it as energizing, mobilizing and transforming as I and many other Artist-Disciples already have. We all have a lot of exciting work to do. Best wishes to you as we embark on this Artist-Disciple journey together. *"It's time..."*

Section I: Vision

Lesson 1:
The Vision of Artist-Discipleship

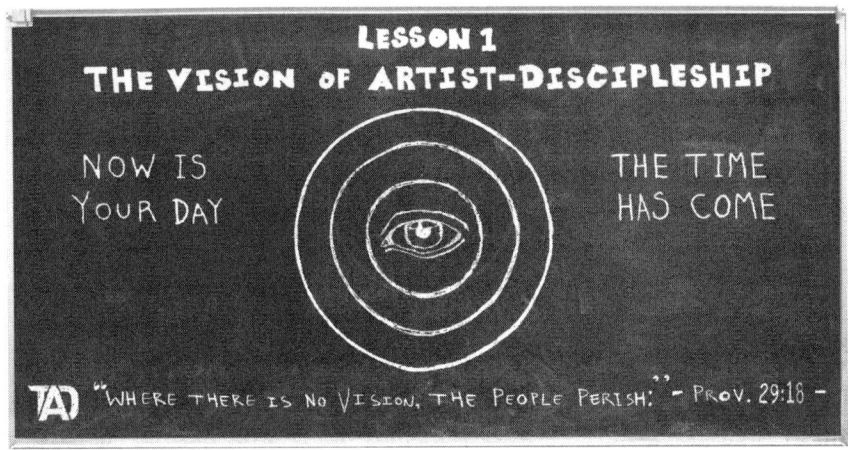

Welcome to the Team

Greetings, and welcome to *The Artist-Disciple* movement. My name is Brydon Brett and I'd like to congratulate you for picking up this book. You are about to meet "an idea whose time has come,"[1] to embark on a journey that could transform your life, and to become part of a team that will help change the world. Art changes lives, and when lives shift, so does everything else.

You are joined in this journey by a global community of Artist-Disciples from many different backgrounds. This book is for each of us. As I've listened to Artist-Disciples in TAD (*The Artist-Disciple*) classes from around the world, I find a common desire to transform through the arts. Here is what some of us are saying:

> *I want to develop a greater understanding of the creative process, improve my ability to motivate myself in creative endeavors, and gain insight into the role of creativity and artistry in the Church, the gospel of Jesus Christ, and the plan of salvation.* – Bryan

> *The question I ask for myself is, "What will my creative imprint be when I leave this earth life and did I do what I came here to*

do?"...I never want to forget who I am and why I am here. — Kamian

I hope [to] discover my creative work. I know that it is in me somewhere. — Solangie

I hope to learn how to remove some of the blocks which have stinted my creative work so far. I hope to learn some habits which can help me flesh out my creative work a little more specifically. I hope to live up to my privilege, my birthright, as a covenant daughter of the Creator. — Rachel

I hope to be more open and honestly critical about my creative work. I want to set goals that I can accomplish and that will help me get to my ultimate [goals]. I want to be more fastidious about doing the things I set out to do, and more perfectly access God's guidance in my creative work. — Kristina

I would like to solidify change, and change even more for the better. I feel empowered by the incredible people that have been, are, and surely those who will be involved in this [work] and community. True Artist-Disciples...give me courage to work harder and be better. — Kendra

What is an Artist-Disciple?
Simply put, an Artist-Disciple is a member of the Church of Jesus Christ of Latter-day Saints or any other denomination who desires to use their creative gifts on purpose to build the kingdom of God on earth. Because this book is primarily designed for a Latter-day Saint audience, the language used and many of the examples given will be from this perspective. However, Artist-Disciples welcome believers and transformational artists from many backgrounds.

I like to describe the project itself this way:

> *The purpose of <u>The Artist-Disciple</u> project is to encourage, educate, inspire, and mobilize the LDS creative community. The ultimate goal of the project is to empower Artist-Disciples around the world to use their creative gifts to build up the Kingdom of God and prepare the earth for the Second Coming of Jesus Christ.*

If that sounds like you, you are an Artist-Disciple. At this point, though, some of you may be asking another question.

Am I an artist?

For many of you, this answer is easy. You are graphic designers and painters, musicians and entertainers, authors and poets, architects and sculptors, vocal percussionists and vocalists, pianists and violinists, music therapists and music teachers, lighting directors and stage managers, YouTube superstars and web programmers, film actors and stage actors. The term "artist" fits naturally.

If you don't feel you fit into the categories above and find yourself questioning how the term applies to you, consider this: because it is our nature to create, we are all artists in some way. If your life's work involves creation of any sort, you are an artist, and you belong to a global team of artists and creators. Artist-Disciples include preparing and returned missionaries, marketing directors and salesmen, educators and public speakers, stay-at-home mothers, working single mothers and many other fields, pursuits and lifestyles.

So I'm an Artist-Disciple, now what?

Now, we have work to do. We live in a time when the best in every field of endeavor is coming forth to change the hearts and minds of people in preparation for the Second Coming of Jesus Christ and His Millennial reign. A vital part of this process is the arts, especially because they have an unparalleled power to reach to the very core of our being. Did you know that prophets have prophesied for hundreds of years about what we can accomplish as artists and disciples at this time in history? Do you understand your place in this? Why is it important for you to catch a vision of Artist-Discipleship?

First of all, understanding our power as a creator can have a dramatic impact on everyday life. A wise man once told me that a seer is someone who, looking down the hallway, can see around the corner. As people who are creating lives as artists, we want to know what is coming for us and how we can best enjoy the present and prepare for the future.

Second, Oliver Wendell Holmes once said, "Man's mind once stretched by a new idea, never regains its original dimensions."[2] Too many of us may have been playing too small, without realizing the kind of impact we could be having on our families and the world. A vision of where we are going will stretch our minds past their original dimensions and help us not just to *see* possibilities, but to *feel* our direction.

Third, the ancient prophet Ammon taught that "...a seer can know of things which are past, and also of things which are to come."[3] It is important to believe that the things the prophets have to say actually will come to pass and then do everything in our power to assist in that process. As you read this section and throughout the book, I invite you to have pen and paper handy to take notes of the impressions that come to you while you read.

So what are the prophets saying?

Take a look at these inspiring quotations about the gospel vision of the arts from prophets, seers, revelators, and other leaders acting under the spirit of prophecy and revelation and see if you don't feel a spark of vision and prophecy yourself:

You mark my words, and write them down and see if they do not come to pass. You will see the day that Zion will be far ahead of the outside world in everything pertaining to learning of every kind as we are today in regard to religious matters. God expects Zion to become the praise and glory of the whole earth, so that kings hearing of her fame will come and gaze upon her glory. – John Taylor[4]

We shall yet have Miltons and Shakespeares of our own. God's ammunition is not exhausted. His highest spirits are held in reserve for the latter times. In God's name and by His help we will build up a literature whose tops will touch the heaven, though its foundation may now be low on the earth. – Orson F. Whitney[5]

The greatest poems are not yet written, nor the paintings finished. The greatest hymns and anthems of the Restoration are yet to be composed. The sublimest renditions of them are yet to be conducted. We move forward much slower than need be... – Boyd K. Packer[6]

In our world, there have risen brilliant stars in drama, music, literature, sculpture, painting, science, and all the graces. For long years I have had a vision of members of the Church greatly increasing their already strong positions of excellence till the eyes of all the world will be upon us....Our day, our time, our people, our generation, should produce such, as we catch the total vision of our potential and dream dreams and see visions of the future. –Spencer W. Kimball[7]

If we strive for perfection—the best and greatest—and are never satisfied with mediocrity, we can excel. In the field of both composition and performance, why cannot someone write a greater oratorio than Handel's Messiah*? The best has not yet been composed nor produced.* –Spencer W. Kimball[8]

Every accomplishment, every polished grace, every useful attainment in mathematics, music, and in all sciences and art belong to the Saints –Brigham Young[9]

We call upon all members, those in the arts and those seeking to appreciate the message of good art, to expand their vision of what can be done. If we are going to fill the world with goodness and truth, then we must be worthy to receive inspiration so we can bless the lives of our Heavenly Father's children –M. Russell Ballard[10]

Go to, then, you who are gifted; cultivate your gift. Develop it in any of the arts and in every worthy example of them. If you have the ability and the desire, seek a career or employ your talent as an avocation or cultivate it as a hobby. But in all ways bless others with it. Set a standard of excellence. Employ it in the secular sense to every worthy advantage, but never use it profanely. Never express your gift unworthily. Increase our spiritual heritage in music, in art, in literature, in dance, in drama. When we have done it our activities will be a standard to the world. –Boyd K. Packer[11]

As modern-day Artist-Disciples, that is a little of what we have in store for us. Are you one of those meant to participate in the fulfillment of these prophecies? I hope these quotations inspire you as they do me. As I read, I feel the Holy Spirit expanding my mind and soul, and I find myself wanting to go and make a difference now. I feel ready to do my part in bringing to fruition the greatest dispensation in history, and the advent of our Savior once again on the earth.

Marked Generation

Do you sense who you are and the special role you are to play in this last dispensation? We are the "marked generation" President Ezra Taft Benson was referring to when he taught:

> *For nearly six thousand years, God has...saved for the final inning some of his strongest children, who will help bear off the kingdom triumphantly. And that is where you come in, for you are the generation that must be prepared to meet your God...Make no mistake about it—you are a marked generation. There has never been more expected of the faithful in such a short period of time as there is of us. The final outcome is certain—the forces of righteousness will win...Will we be true to our last-days foreordained mission?*[12]

If you feel an eternal spark awakening you to your divine potential as a creator, don't snuff it out. As I ponder these concepts, I like to keep a study journal handy to record the thoughts and feelings that come to me about my place in history and how I can be true to my foreordained missions to help Zion become the praise and glory of the whole earth. I hope that you choose to do the same.

The Mormon Moment...has just begun

It is clear that we have a lot of work to do and high expectations to live up to. To me, this is a very joyful and inspiring thought. Zion is to become the praise and glory of the whole earth. It is becoming apparent that many of these prophecies are already in process of fulfillment. What the media has dubbed "The Mormon Moment" is already upon us.

Never before in the history of the Church have we been under such a microscope or in such a spotlight. With this attention comes opportunity. Many members of the Church have risen to prominence and influence in their respective fields and it seems to be just the beginning. Of this "Mormon Moment" New York Times best-selling author Stephen Mansfield wrote, "…there is much more to come."[13] As the talent pool in the Church grows, we will continue to strengthen our already strong positions of excellence. We have every reason to believe that we can and will fulfill all that is expected of us in preparation for the Second Coming.

In addition to the Latter-day Saints, many others will get to participate in this unfolding movement as well. Orson F. Whitney said, "God is using more than one people for the accomplishment of his great and marvelous work. The Latter-day Saints cannot do it all. It is too vast, too arduous, for any one people."[14] What an exciting thing to think that we have a chance to work with good people of all faiths and walks of life to accomplish the Lord's work.

Sören Kierkegaard said, "A possibility is a hint from God. One must follow it."[15] Are you sensing a swell of excitement for your place in this "Moment"? What possibilities have been hinted to you?

My Vision

I'm Brydon Brett, just another Artist-Disciple like you. I get onstage every day and try to live what the prophets are teaching. I teach and facilitate *The Artist Disciple* (TAD) classes to inspire others to make a difference as a creator and live up to our potential. As I work both on and off the stage, I can see that what the prophets have said is already beginning to come to pass. Because of my experiences and as part of my personal life mission, I also have a vision. May I share it with you?

I have a vision for us as Artist-Disciples of the world, and the change that is going to happen in the lives of people around us as we decide to step up and live our destiny. I believe that the prophets mean what they say, and I believe that it will happen. I see Artist-Disciples, individually and collectively fulfilling their purpose as they overcome fear, doubt, limitation and insecurities. I see the improvement of communities, the raising of the standard of living globally as the airwaves, the walls, the pages, and the screens of society are filled with inspired, values-based works from Artist-Disciples the world over.

I believe that we are entering into a golden age of creation and that Artist-Disciples have been saved for this time to play a special role in helping craft and transform the world in preparation for the Second Coming of Jesus Christ, as we will continue to discuss throughout this book. I know that there is a lot of opposition. I know that there are critics and cynics and non-believers. I know that Satan is marshaling his forces in formidable and unprecedented ways. I know that there are a lot of challenges that would suggest to our natural eye that we should just give up. But I see nothing in the scriptures, hear nothing in the teachings of the Brethren, and feel nothing in my heart that tells me we're going to lose.

We are on the winning team. And not just the winning team in a painstaking, onerous and miserable battle, but the winning team in an exciting journey filled with prosperity, abundance and joy for Artist-Disciples who have the faith and personal vision to carry out the prophetic vision.

I see people being fulfilled and energized as they work with the Lord to fulfill their personal missions. I see Artist-Disciples mobilizing people of all faiths to fill the world with goodness and truth. I see Artist-Disciples receiving revelation, coming together in dynamic teams, topping the charts, garnering awards, rising to the top of their fields and becoming all that God created them to be. That is my vision for me, and for you, and it is time we do it.

So how do we do it?

Can you *feel* the vision? You are not intended to be mediocre. You can do all things through Christ because He strengthens you.[16] In fact, "If you live up to your privileges, the angels cannot be restrained from being your associates."[17] Right now is the greatest time in the history of our world. We are on the cusp of great things. We live in the days prophesied by Joel:

> *And it shall come to pass…that I will pour out my spirit upon all flesh; and your sons and your daughters shall prophesy, your old men shall dream dreams, your young men shall see visions: And also upon the servants and upon the handmaids in those days will I pour out my spirit.*[18]

This book is an attempt to begin to answer the question "How?" What are the key components and pieces we need to change the world as Artist-Disciples? As we increase our vision, as we are in tune to the "music of faith,"[19] and as we keep our mind "continually on the stretch after the things of God,"[20] we will eventually compose the greatest anthems yet to be written and "dance to forms of music yet to be heard."[21] Now is our day. This is the time. Why not us? Why not now?

> **Questions and Action Items:**
>
> 1. What is the Lord's view of your potential? Is it greater than your own?
>
> 2. What is your personal vision? If nothing stood in your way, what is the biggest thing you could ever hope to accomplish?
>
> 3. What is the price to be paid to finish this goal?
>
> 4. What are the gifts, tools, and talents you bring to accomplishing this goal?
>
> 5. What impact could your vision and goals have on the Kingdom of God?

Chapter Summary

- By virtue of your creative nature and individual mission in life, you are an artist, and as you choose to pursue a life as a disciple of Jesus Christ, you are also an Artist-Disciple.
- Prophets and Church leaders have laid out an inspiring vision of our day and the special role the arts will play in preparing for the Second Coming.
- You and I are part of a prophecy-fulfilling generation of Artist-Disciples destined to help Zion become the praise and glory of the whole earth.
- Because the "Mormon Moment" is upon us and will only increase in intensity, we have a unique opportunity to hasten the work of the Lord by stepping up and fulfilling our roles on the Lord's team.

[1] Rosemary Okolo, *Dare to Shine!: Making Positive Changes in a Negative World.* EBook.
[2] Oliver Wendell Holmes, quotationspage.com/quote/26186.html.
[3] Mosiah 8:17.
[4] John Taylor, Sermon, September 20, 1857; see *The Messenger,* July 1953, as quoted by Spencer W. Kimball, "Education for Eternity," BYU Annual Faculty Conference, September 12, 1967.
[5] Orson F. Whitney, Lecture delivered at YMMIA conference, 3 June 1888, as quoted by Boyd K. Packer, "The Arts and the Spirit of the Lord," BYU Fireside, February 01, 1976.
[6] Boyd K. Packer, "The Arts and the Spirit of the Lord," BYU Fireside, February 01, 1976.
[7] Spencer W. Kimball, "The Gospel Vision of the Arts," *Ensign,* July 1977.
[8] Kimball, "The Gospel Vision of the Arts," *Ensign,* July 1977.
[9] Brigham Young as quoted by Spencer W. Kimball, "The Gospel Vision of the Arts," *Ensign,* July 1977.
[10] M. Russell Ballard, "Filling the World with Goodness and Truth," *Ensign,* July 1996.
[11] Packer, "The Arts and the Spirit of the Lord," BYU Fireside, February 01, 1976.
[12] Ezra Taft Benson, *Teachings of Ezra Taft Benson: Achieving Your Life Mission,* 105.
[13] Stephen Mansfield, "The Mormonizing of America," huffingtonpost.com/stephen-mansfield/the-mormonizing-of-americ_b_2083125.html.
[14] Orson F. Whitney, "Too Vast, Too Arduous, For Any One People," in Conference Report, April 1928, 59.
[15] Sören Kierkegaard, *The Soul of Kierkegaard: Selections from His Journals,* 147.
[16] Philippians 4:13.
[17] Joseph Smith, as quoted by James E. Faust, "How Near to the Angels," *New Era,* March 1999.
[18] Joel 2:28-29.
[19] Quentin L. Cook, "In Tune with the Music of Faith," *Ensign,* May 2012.
[20] John Taylor, as quoted by The Church of Jesus Christ of Latter-day Saints, *Teachings of Presidents of the Church: John Taylor,* 97-105.
[21] Warren G. Bennis, brainyquote.com/quotes/quotes/w/warrengbe121710.html.

Lesson 2:
The Power

Artist-Disciple Insights

Rachel's Story: Magnify My Desire

As I was listening to the words of Elder Holland, he said something which sparked an idea in me...He said something about children singing "I'm Trying to Be Like Jesus," and almost as an afterthought added, "Overlaid with 'I Am a Child of God.'"

This apostle ignited an idea which swelled and grew until I had the outlines of a medley in my hand. Imagine two people singing together about how the truths that they are children of God and their attempts to be like Jesus are interwoven...I'm amazed at how even the smallest afterthought can be inspired of the Lord. I was not in the audience to whom Elder Holland was speaking, but the Lord knew that I would be touched to watch this question-and-answer session; and after pledging to do His will, He knew I would be ready to flesh out this tremendous idea.

It is through the Spirit that we receive inspiration—as artists, as servants, as children. But even so, it is only when we are willing to act upon that inspiration in whatever small capacity we have that we are given such inspiration. And He can magnify any talent, any desire, and any attempt so that it works together for your good and for the good of His work and His glory, even the bringing to pass the immortality and eternal life of His children.

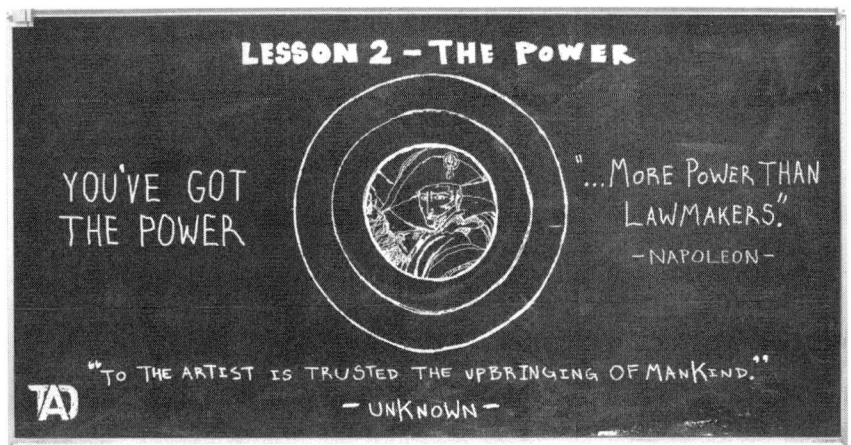

Why do Artist-Disciples matter?

Think for a moment of all the "art" you came in contact with today. If a notebook or electronic device is handy, you may want to jot down a few answers so you can see it even more clearly. For instance, what did you listen to, look at, or read? Next, how did these impact you? What messages came to you through lyrics, images, words, and symbols?

Got it?

Now ponder: what is the collective effect of music, movies, art, literature, photography, teaching, speaking, marketing, or any of the arts on you and those closest to you? At the next level, what is the effect of these same things on your neighborhood, city, community, and world?

Do the arts really have that much power?

If you are still not quite sure, consider this: what if all the art in the world as it now is suddenly stopped tomorrow? No more music, TV, novels, dancing, paintings…What would happen to nations? How would families react or interact? What would *you* do?

President George Albert Smith said, "I wonder sometimes if we realize the importance of music. I wonder if we know that the Lord himself is concerned about it…"[1]

Why would the Lord be concerned about music and the arts? Why do you think the medium of artistic creation has such power?

My hope is for us to begin to have some idea of what the arts have done and continue to do to change—and create—the world. As we discuss this topic, please be aware that I am thinking of all the arts, from pottery to publishing to planting a garden. However, because I am a musician by profession, much of the research presented in this lesson has to do with the power of music. Let it be noted, however, that similar things could be said of all other forms of artistic creation.

In what ways do the arts impact us?

In this lesson we will examine the power of art in emotions and spirituality, in building communities, in shaping our minds, and even its influence on culture and policy-making. I hope that we will all take special note of what each of these areas means to each of us every day. More than being a reflector of society, art so often becomes its director. Most especially, the art you create influences *you* toward what is ultimately *your* destiny.

Emotional Power of Art

It is well-known that the arts are used to communicate feelings and emotions. Catholic Bishop Alexander Mileant said this about music, but it's applicable across all the arts:

> *Music is one of the most inspirational forms of fine art. In its rhythm, melody, harmony and dynamics, its variety of sounds, shades and nuances, music transmits a never-ending gamut of feelings and sensations. Its power is contained in its ability to by-pass reason, penetrating straight into the soul, into the subconscious, and to manipulate a person's feelings. Depending on its content, music can evoke the most elevated and noble feelings, such as assisting in creating empathy for prayer—or produce quite the opposite, by arousing the most sinful and base desires.[2]*

There are physical, neurological, and spiritual reasons why music has the power to evoke such emotion. The prophet Joseph Smith taught:

> *Man of himself is an instrument of music; and when the chords of which he is composed are touched, and salute the ear, the sounds appeal to his spirit and the sentiment to his understanding. If the strains are harmonious, he endorses and enjoys them with supreme delight; whether the tones are from a human voice or from an instrument, they arrest his attention and absorb his whole being.[3]*

Hundreds of scientific studies have been done that back up these statements. How could a study of this research add depth and understanding to your use of the arts? A simple online search will get you started, and from there you will find plenty more to add breadth and scholarly research to aid your understanding.

For now, it is sufficient to understand that music and the arts have real power over human emotions and can influence our moods and behaviors. As Bishop Mileant put it, "Music is part of us, and it either ennobles or degrades our behavior."[4]

Lex de Azevedo, an LDS composer, said it this way:

> *Words communicate ideas. Music communicates feelings. While words get stuck in the thinking part of our brain, music sails*

through to reach the innermost corners of our emotional being, thereby governing lives and actions…This is precisely why music is such a wonderful, dangerous, exciting power…[5]

Spiritual Power of Art

Art also has great spiritual power. Since spiritual and temporal are so interrelated, this should come as no surprise. President Boyd K. Packer said, "We are able to feel and learn very quickly through music, through art, through poetry, some spiritual things that we would otherwise learn very slowly."[6]

Think about this for a moment. If we are inherently creators, and we are here on this earth to learn some important things about creating, shouldn't we pay close attention to anything that can aid us in that process? Could designing a welcoming home, capturing a thought provoking image, or choreographing a combination of movement or sounds help prepare us for eternal work? Indeed it seems that art has the power to bypass the intellect and go straight to the heart, and even to speed up the learning process that is the very purpose for our being on this earth. If we fully understood this concept, I believe we would participate in and invest ourselves much more earnestly in art, both in its creation and in our enjoyment of it. There are deep implications behind these concepts that are worth our pondering and consideration.

Kevin's Story

I have witnessed personally the power of art and its ability to influence an individual spiritually. When I served as Young Men president in our ward, I knew one young man since he entered the program as a deacon. We will call him Kevin. When Kevin became a member of the Young Men, he was one of our most conscientious, innocent and dutiful deacons—always on time to pass the sacrament, always attending his meetings, and fully living the standards of the church. His single mother told me that he was the same way at home—organizing family prayer, helping around the house, and listening to spiritual and uplifting music.

Kevin's older brother was a priest and we could never get him to come to activities or participate in any way in the gospel. Eventually he decided to leave home before graduating high school, sever his relationship with his mother, and distance himself completely from the standards of the Church. Kevin did not condone his brother's actions, and when his brother was still at home, he defended his mother against his brother's disrespect and took on the role of spiritual leader in the home.

Right before Kevin turned fourteen, he and his mother moved out of our ward for a few months. When they moved back into our ward boundary, I noticed a change in Kevin. He was still a great young man with a righteous nature, but something was changing.

Seeking to nip the problem in the bud, I approached Kevin and learned that he had started listening to screamo and metal music, which, not coincidentally, were the same kinds of music his brother had participated in. Knowing what I know about the power of music in spirituality, emotions, and behavior, I gave him a friendly, yet stern, warning that this would lead to trouble. He didn't listen.

Over time, Kevin distanced himself from his quorum members, from his family, and from the Church. His mother told me that he started locking himself in his room with headphones so he could listen to his music. Since initially writing this story and compiling in my notes for this book, Kevin has also left home, defriended his own mother on Facebook, and won't return my phone calls. I don't consider music to be the sole reason for Kevin's spiritual decline, but it is clear that music and the arts have tremendous spiritual and emotional power—

enough to alter our moods, behaviors, lifestyles and spiritual orientation.

Community-building Power of Art

> *[It is] precisely during celebrations and singing events [that] we have an excellent opportunity to have a political effect wide beyond the typical. Formation songs possess the strongest community-building power. Thus we use them deliberately at those moments when we want to waken the consciousness of being part of a community, in order to deepen the power of such an experience.[7]*

In slightly different language, the above quotation could have been used to describe many experiences you and I have on a regular basis—ball games, pop concerts, school assemblies, even church gatherings. What makes it particularly interesting is that it is from an Official HJ (Hitler Jugend or Hitler Youth) Memo during World War II.

It should be no surprise to us, knowing the power of music in our lives, to discover that the Hitler regime used music to train the youth of the Reich. According to one research team:

> *Group singing was considered particularly important as a means of building group cohesion and obedience, and numerous songbooks were published for this purpose. Ironically, these activities integrated many musical practices common to banned communist and leftist youth groups—the emphasis on group music-making rather than solo performances, the importance of folk songs, the use of music to build group solidarity—and often used the very same songs, simply changing the lyrics to promote a Nazi world view.[8]*

Have you noticed how the power of music builds unity and community in small and large groups? Music and art can create devoted followers more quickly and often more permanently than almost anything else.

As American writer Henry Theodore Tuckerman puts it, "Explain it as we may, a martial strain will urge a man into the front rank of battle sooner than an argument, and a fine anthem excite his devotion more certainly than a logical discourse."[9]

This community-building power of music and art can be extremely positive. Some of my most tender memories have to do with singing in choirs or groups where a feeling of love and unity was magnified by the music in such a powerful way as to leave an indelible impression on my soul. Perhaps you have experienced a similar thing with your music. Harriet A. Seymour said this:

> *Music makes anything go. It makes a peace meeting more peaceful, it intensifies the spirit of courage in soldiers, it makes drunkards drink more, it seduces, it uplifts, it stimulates workers, it soothes and it heals. We are to decide its use, destructive or constructive.*[10]

In other words, whatever happens in a group and community, whether positive or negative, is accented, intensified and memorialized by music.

It happened in Kansas City...

Music was used constructively during the youth cultural celebration for the Kansas City, MO, temple dedication, which President Thomas S. Monson referenced in the October 2012 general conference.[11] Over 3,000 youth were in one large room together, eager and excited to sing and perform for the Prophet, who was coming to dedicate the temple and witness their performance.

As one of the stake leaders on the floor, I was in charge of corralling youth and making sure they got to their spots on time during pre-performance rehearsals. I experienced many of the same challenges the other leaders did. The noise of youth talking to each other was so loud that the cultural celebration committee chairman could not even be heard over the sound system. This persisted for a couple of hours.

Observing the loudness and chaos in the room, a wise leader leaned over to me and said, "If they'd just have the kids sing a hymn it would solve the problem." I mentioned this idea to someone who had more sway than I did and he may have passed it up the line. In any case, at the request of the chairman, the beautiful strains of "I Love to See the Temple" began to make their way above the clamor.

Eventually all 3,000 youth and leaders joined in and there was peace enough for the committee to communicate their instructions. Later on, as the youth sang with one voice and one heart to the Prophet, there was a powerful feeling of love and Zion that I will never forget. Lives were changed that night through the power of the Spirit and through the community-building power of music.

Mind-altering Power of Art

Have you noticed how your thoughts after you come out of a concert or movie are different than when you went into it? Have you ever turned on a playlist to help you study?

In the early 1900s, the great opera composer Pietro Mascagni added his view, "Modern music is as dangerous as narcotics."[12] Indeed, anything that has the power to alter our mental state is dangerous. Tolstoy said it somewhat poetically:

> *A terrible thing is music in general…Music makes me forget my real situation. It transports me into a state which is not my own. Under the influence of music I really seem to feel what I do not understand, to have powers which I cannot have.*[13]

Michael Ballam once observed that the "Greeks wouldn't allow music or poems set to rhythm (like rap music) because of the power it had to imprint messages and ideas in the minds of the people."[14] Bishop Alexander Mileant said it somewhat more scientifically by explaining how our brains are susceptible to the influence of music and adds:

> *Excitation and melancholy can be created by music/sensory overload...Any time you overload the mind, the person becomes very suggestible. They will take in anything that you suggest at that time because they have no defenses against it. People can walk out of concerts in a hyper-suggestible state...Music has a tendency to defuse thinking and create moods. And in turn, the messages seep in.*[15]

While music and art have significant effects on the physical body and physical world—numerous studies have shown the impact of certain styles of music on everything from plants to snowflakes to tomatoes—perhaps the most significant thing about the physical effects of music is that the sensory overload of many types of music weakens the mind and makes it susceptible to messages. This opens the door to moral and societal changes of a much broader nature.

Cultural and Policy-Making Power of Art

Imagine for a moment that you had the ability to choose a song that would be played in every home in your nation once a day, every day. What would you choose? How would you select from the variety of melodies and lyrics? What message would you want to be broadcast to *your* family daily?

Thoughts are the starting point of all action. The arts influence thoughts first, which inform morals, or the code by which actions are measured. Consistent actions, influenced by morals, determine long-term behavior; and when behavior is spread, it becomes the culture of individuals, families and nations. Culture then ultimately writes the laws. One writer wrote about the negative cultural effects of the rock and roll movement in this way:

> *Songs used to have a moral message. But today's music is often amoral, advocating an anything goes, no-holds-barred type of lifestyle. Rock and roll has, as predicted, lead to a culture of immorality and debauchery.*[16]

Other thinkers and historical figures have spoken to these points as well. Did you know that they had things like this to say?

> *Any musical innovation is full of danger to the whole State… [W]hen modes of music change, the fundamental laws of the State always change with them.* –Plato[17]

> *Musicians have more power than law-makers.* –Napoleon Bonaparte[18]

> *For changing people's manners and altering their customs, there is nothing better than music.* –Shu Ching[19]

> *I knew a very wise man who believed that if a man were permitted to make all the ballads, he need not care who should make the laws of a nation.* –Andrew Fletcher[20]

> *The life of the arts, far from being an interruption, a distraction, in the life of a nation, is close to the center of a nation's purpose, and is a test of the quality of a nation's civilization.* –John F. Kennedy[21]

What is the quality of your nation's civilization? If it is demonstrated in its arts, what does it say about the direction we are going? Do we have reason to be alarmed?

Are you a puppet?

Here in the USA, over 90% of our media is controlled by only six companies.[22] I am not a conspiracy theorist or a doomsday prophet by any means, but it is clear to me that the arts have more influence on our lives than we realize. Do our youth get their education more from the screen or their headphones than they do from the pulpit? What messages are transmitted across the airwaves to our children? Whose kingdom is being built by these messages? To whom are we and our youth listening—the Lord, or the adversary? Has Satan succeeded in enrolling us in the University of Babylon?

Elder David R. Stone said:

> *Our culture tends to determine what foods we like, how we dress, what constitutes polite behavior, what sports we should follow, what our taste in music should be, the importance of education, and our attitudes toward honesty. It also influences men as to the importance of recreation or religion, influences women about the priority of career or childbearing, and has a powerful effect on how we approach procreation and moral issues. All too often, we are like puppets on a string, as our culture determines what is "cool."*[23]

Artists like to justify the morality of some of their creations by saying, "I'm just reflecting real life and how society really is." But the reality is that *society reflects art*. Art is more often than not the engine that drives ideas into the individual and public consciousness which, in turn, develops the culture and, ultimately, the laws of a society.

The Power and Responsibility of the Artist

Are you beginning to feel the potential impact of an Artist-Disciple?

Artists are the vehicles through which art is created. They are the practitioners, the technicians, the organizers of a medium that literally shapes our world every day. It should not surprise us that artists are among the most powerful and influential figures in society, even if it's not generally recognized. As an artist, you can have a far-reaching effect on lives and nations.

What a contrast this is to the perception that is so often placed on artists today. "When are you going to quit that music thing and get a real job?" I've had many people ask me this question or imply it. The "starving artist" stereotype can be a hard one to get past in the "real world."

Equally hard to overcome is the stereotype that all artists are attention-starved, spotlight-hungry, sensationalist, flamboyant and egocentric. I love what Stephen Pressfield had to say about this latter stereotype:

> *Creative work is not a selfish act or a bid for attention on the part of the actor. It's a gift to the world and every being in it. Don't cheat us of your contribution. Give us what you've got.*[24]

What is it that you have to share? Don't cheat us of it. As Artist-Disciples, you and I view our creative work as an offering or a mission, something to give to the world. It is likely that we will sometimes be misunderstood in our intentions. Still, we must never forget the real place of an artist, and the incredible power we have to shape the ideas and culture of the world.

What is your strategy?

Like many artists in the world today, you may, until now, have been more or less unconscious of your power. This is not the case with many of the "big names" in the world of art. Some know exactly what they're doing. For instance, famous rock guitarist Jimi Hendrix said, "You can hypnotize people with music and when you get them at their weakest point, you can preach into the subconscious what we want to say."²⁵ Mr. Hendrix obviously understood what he was using his art to do, and how to do it.

Sam Phillips, the man responsible for launching Elvis Presley's career, said, "The greats...be it of country, rhythm & blues, rock 'n' roll...you know what they were doing? They were messing with your heart and soul. That's what it was. Nothing has the strength, the power of music."²⁶

Taking this to another level, Michael Ballam shared an experience that Gene Cook had with Mick Jagger of the Rolling Stones, arguably one of the most influential musicians of all time. Brother Cook found himself sitting on an airplane next to Mick. At first he didn't know who he was, but Mr. Jagger quickly let him know. Brother Ballam picks up the story from there:

> *At that point, my friend Gene Cook said, "Ya' know, Mick, I have the opportunity to be with a lot of young people across this nation and many of them say your music does not affect them adversely or in any way for that matter. But others say that your music affects them in a very bad way. What is your opinion on that, Mr. Jagger? What do you believe your impact is and why do you do it?"*
>
> *Mick Jagger said, "Our music is calculated to drive kids to sex." [Brother Cook] said, "Excuse me, could you repeat that?" "Our music is calculated to drive kids to sex. It's not our fault what they do, you know? It's up to them. But we can make a lot of money doing that," he said. He was just coming from Mexico where he had made some films for MTV. The reason he had gone to Mexico was that a) it was cheaper, and b) he could portray anything he chose to portray on the screen. He knew that some of it, at this point, would not be let on American television yet. But the day would come when they could expose anything sexually, anything violently that they chose to, and believe me, Mr. Jagger proposes to, or so he told my friend Gene Cook.*

> *Now, he said something else about all of this. He said that their music had another purpose…My friend Gene said, "Mick, why do you do this? What motivates you to fly all over the country and do all of this? It's not the money because, as I understand it, you're pretty wealthy." Mick said, "Never be able to spend the money I've got." "Is it the power of being able to influence people by your popularity? Do you need this for your ego?" Mick said, "Oh no, it's the power to influence the youth of the world."*
>
> *And then I quote what he said in TIME magazine in 1969: "We are moving after the minds of the young people of the world…to tell them that the world is a rotten place, that there is no hope, that they have to take, that there are no rules in life. Our job here is to take what we can take."*[27]

Not all artists are so transparent about their strategy and most, including Mr. Jagger, don't wear it on their sleeve. This was a *private* conversation Mick had with Gene Cook. In *public* practice, the strategy is slick and appealing, making evil look good and good look evil[28] until fans are lulled away into carnal security and Satan grasps them with his awful chains.[29]

President Packer said, "There have always been those who take the beautiful things and corrupt them. It's happened with nature; it's happened with literature, drama, art; and it certainly has happened with music."[30]

Not every artist has a strategy like Mick Jagger, but certainly we, as Artist-Disciples, could benefit from developing strategy and purpose around our creative work. Can we be as active for righteousness as Mr. Jagger and others are for wickedness? I believe that you and I don't need to be a part of that crowd. We can stand for truth and righteousness in what we create. If they can harness the power of art for evil, then we can harness it for good. I also believe that it is our responsibility to do this. Niu Ta'ala, of the songwriting team Ivoga Green and Niu Ta'ala, said,

> *Some of the world's music is wonderful. But too much of it portrays evil to be something good or inevitable—even normal. Not all battles are fought on a battlefield. And not all soldiers dress in camouflage. Ivoga and I join forces with others doing what we can in our part of the vineyard to combat evil through the talent we have been given. Gifts come with responsibility, and we are well aware of that.*[31]

As Artist-Disciples, you and I have been given gifts, talents and abilities. And, since art is meant to be experienced, we've also been given a platform—some bigger and more public than others, but platforms nonetheless. "For of him unto whom much is given much is required…"[32] The Artist-Disciple, as an agent of influence in society, has the responsibility to teach truth in his or her creation. Do you have a strategy to do so?

A Word of Warning: The Power of Art over Us

Once, when I was swimming in the ocean along the Gulf Coast, I swam so far out into the ocean that the waves began to pull me outward away from the shore rather than pushing me toward the shore. There were no lifeguards and I began to fear for my life. It took all my strength, prayers and willpower to overcome the current and the waves and finally make it back to shore. When I hit dry ground I looked all around for my friends, but our camp was nowhere to be found. I finally found them but only after walking over half a mile back down the beach. I hadn't even realized that I'd drifted that far. It was easy to be pulled away from camp when I lost sight of it and swam in dangerous areas.

As I have worked with Artist-Disciples from around the world, I find that our experience navigating the artistic world is much like this story. The current of the arts is strong, and there are many temptations along the way.

For instance, artists tend to be more visible than the average person, more recognized and applauded. We may feel more "called" than others, and because we tend to think of artists as role models and influencers in society, we also may tend to think that our artistic gifts are somehow more important than other people's gifts.

More dangerously, we sometimes might think that our artistic gifts constitute a mission or offering purely because we have them. Or, even worse, we might consider our artistic gifts to be our "calling," hence no need for a priesthood calling or an eternal calling like motherhood. An inflated perception of our own importance will only prove a stumbling block in our goal of Kingdom-building and impacting the world for good. What *is* true is that artists do have great power and responsibility. If there's anything that sets us apart, it is that truth. We must be careful that the power of art that we are trying to wield for good does not overtake our lives for bad.

Additionally, there is often great pressure associated with being an artist and too often we see tragic examples of artists who turn to unworthy means to handle it, losing their lives and often their souls in the process. In all of these associated challenges, it is crucial to keep our eye focused and single to the glory of God.

"Be back by midnight"

I remember talking with a returned missionary who was going into the field of film acting. I could tell that he felt immune to temptation, but that he was also very naïve about the morally treacherous world he was getting in to. I felt an attitude from him of, "Oh, that could never happen to me." It reminded me of this story about President J. Reuben Clark Jr. as told by Charles Dahlquist II in a general conference address. His teenage daughter was getting ready to leave for a dance, when they had this conversation:

He said, "Have fun, my dear. Be back by midnight." She replied, "Daddy, this is the night of the prom. We go to the dance and are not back until early morning." President Clark responded, "Yes, I know that is what many will be doing. But you must be back before midnight." She, then, in desperation said, "Daddy, you just don't trust me!" To which he replied, "My dear, in the wrong place, at the wrong time, I don't even trust myself. Be back by midnight."[33]

This is a helpful reminder for all of us. In all that we do as artists we must constantly "take heed"[34] that we are not overtaken by the power of the Devil, the power of the arts or by what Pat Debenham calls "the seduction of our gifts."[35] We can stay safe by staying away from dangerous areas and always keeping our eyes focused on Christ's camp and our eternal goals.

Your Journey

From Michael Jackson to Monet, from Machiavelli to Mozart—where is art taking you? While there is much darkness in the world today, many are working faithfully to combat forces of evil by seeking to create art full of goodness and truth and reverse some of these negative cultural trends. Slash, of the rock band Guns 'n Roses said, "Whenever society gets too stifling and the rules get too complex, there's some sort of musical explosion."[36] Is it possible that there could be a musical and artistic explosion in a positive direction coming soon?

As an Artist-Disciple, you have widespread and visible opportunities to influence the world. How are you using *your* power?

Questions and Action Items:

1. Describe a time when an experience with art altered your mood in any direction.

2. How can artistic expression inspire or deflate a community, communicate an idea, and move people to action?

3. How would you like to see artistic expression influencing your community?

4. Why would God be concerned about music and the arts?

5. Why do you think artistic creation has such power?

Chapter Summary

- All forms of art have tremendous seen and unseen power to shape the culture, laws and values of society.
- Artists must respect the responsibility and power they have to use the arts and their personal influence to shape culture, laws and values.
- As Artist-Disciples, we would do well to strategize and make sure our creations are in line with our vision and principles.
- Art can have consuming power over us if we allow ourselves to get out of balance.
- Remember, you control the arts, don't let the arts control you.

---

[1] George Albert Smith, *Church News,* February 16, 1946, 6.
[2] Alexander Mileant, "Rock Music, From a Christian Viewpoint," fatheralexander.org/booklets/english/rock_music_e.htm.
[3] Joseph Smith, as quoted by Reid Nibley, "Thoughts on Music in the Church," *Ensign*, February 1972, 13.

[4] Mileant, "Rock Music, From a Christian Viewpoint," fatheralexander.org/booklets/english/rock_music_e.htm.
[5] Lex de Azevedo, *Pop Music & Morality*, 37.
[6] Boyd K. Packer, *Devotional Speeches of the Year (1977)*, 267.
[7] ORT Research Team, "Music and the Holocaust: Music Amongst the Hitler Youth," holocaustmusic.ort.org/politics-and-propaganda/third-reich/music-hitler-youth/.
[8] ORT Research Team, "Music and the Holocaust," holocaustmusic.ort.org/politics-and-propaganda/third-reich/music-hitler-youth/.
[9] Henry Theodore Tuckerman, winwisdom.com/quotes/author/henry-theodore-tuckerman.aspx.
[10] Harriet Ayer Seymour, *What Music Can Do for You*, eBook.
[11] Thomas S. Monson, "Consider the Blessings," *Ensign*, November 2012.
[12] Pietro Mascagni, *Music: A Book of Quotations*, 32.
[13] Leo Tolstoy, as quoted by Lex De Azevedo, *Pop Music & Morality*, 29.
[14] Michael Ballam, *Music and the Mind*, Phoenix Productions, 1994.
[15] Mileant, "Rock Music, From a Christian Viewpoint," fatheralexander.org/booklets/english/rock_music_e.htm.
[16] The Parlor Songs Academy, parlorsongs.com/issues/2006-2/thismonth/feature.php.
[17] Plato, as quoted by Lex de Azevedo, *Pop Music and Morality*, 69.
[18] Napoleon Bonaparte, as quoted by Michael Ballam, *Music and the Mind*, Phoenix Productions, 1994.
[19] Shu Ching, earlymusic.dikmans.net/quotes.html.
[20] Andrew Fletcher, as quoted by Lex de Azevedo, *Pop Music and Morality*, 99.
[21] John F. Kennedy, as quoted by Michael Zager, *Music Production: For Producers, Composers, Arrangers, and Students*, 401.
[22] Ashley Lutz, "These 6 Corporations Control 90% of the Media in America," businessinsider.com/these-6-corporations-control-90-of-the-media-in-america-2012-6.
[23] David R. Stone, "Zion in the Midst of Babylon," *Ensign*, May 2006.
[24] Stephen Pressfield, *Besides the Bible*, 194.
[25] Jimi Hendrix, as quoted by Alexander Mileant, "Rock Music, From a Christian Viewpoint," fatheralexander.org/booklets/english/rock_music_e.htm.
[26] Sam Phillips, gorehound1313.wordpress.com/quotes-of-successful-guitarists/.
[27] Ballam, *Music and the Mind*, Phoenix Productions, 1994.
[28] 2 Nephi 15:20.
[29] 2 Nephi 28:21-22.
[30] Boyd K. Packer, "The Message: Worthy Music, Worthy Thoughts," *New Era*, April 2008.

[31] Niu Ta'ala, as quoted by Nicole Sheahan, "Inside Mormon Music: LDS Music, Kiwified," deseretnews.com/article/705379039/LDS-music-Kiwified.html?pg=all.
[32] Doctrine and Covenants 82:3.
[33] Charles W. Dahlquist ll, "Preparing to Receive the Ordinances of the Temple," *Ensign*, May 2008.
[34] Doctrine and Covenants 20:32-34.
[35] Pat Debenham, "The Seduction of Our Gifts," *BYU Studies Quarterly*, Vol. 41:3.
[36] Slash, uwex.edu/erc/music/quotes.html.

Lesson 3:
The Problem

Artist-Disciple Insights

Diane's Story: Clothing the Emperor

The mediocre offerings of today's entertainment set a dangerous mental precedent much like the mind games so aptly illustrated in the old story of The Emperor's Clothes. More than ever, people today cheer and clap their hands and shell out dollars to hear and see things which have no real worth or substance.

I had occasion recently to think long and hard about this phenomenon when a Facebook artist acquaintance requested clarification regarding a type of matte-finish polyester film. Other artists tried their best to describe the drawing surface with words, but I decided that a picture would do more to help this confused artist. I placed my hand under a sheet of the film and took a photo. The partially see-through image of my hand under the film was effective, and I sent the image to the Facebook group along with a description of what I had done.

Attached comments were forthcoming and surprising. Brilliant…wonderful…amazing…so creative!

As I read the comments, I wondered, "Had I really created something outstanding and artistically 'brilliant?'"

My head began to swell for a moment, but reality took over. The unwarranted applause had to be looked at with a critical eye and, one might say, laughed at for its true absurdity. This was nothing more than The Emperor's Clothes once again!

Yes, the world can change people, and pride can be a terrible stumbling block, but a true Artist-Disciple will accept the challenge to become something real and not just go through the motions no matter how loud the cheers become.

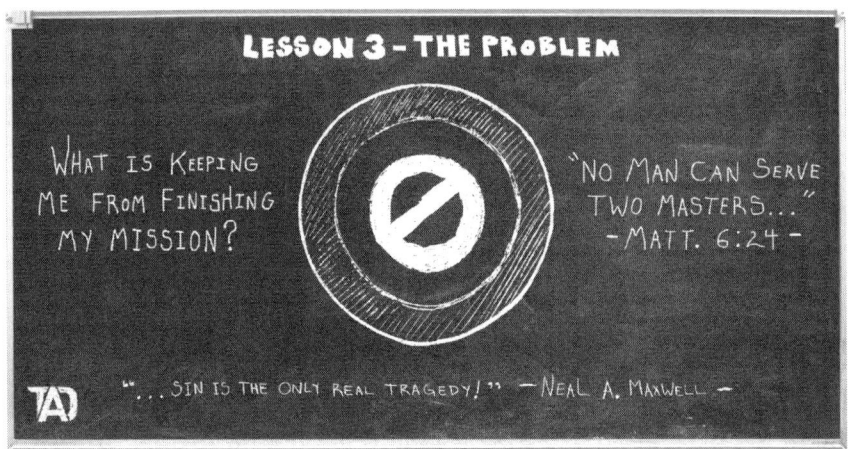

Ready, set…what are we waiting for?

What stops us?

I mean, as Artist-Disciples, we have the opportunity to participate in prophetic vision, and we understand that the arts do have power to change the world. What stops us from topping the charts, hanging paintings at the Louvre, and dramatically impacting the morals and culture of society? If artists have so much power, why isn't our individual art and personal influence more powerful?

As I have worked and studied with Artist-Disciples from many different backgrounds, I have concluded that there are three main challenges, or obstacles, that hold us back from the impact we could be having on individual lives, families, communities, and the world. In discussing these, I hope to paint a picture of the current creative scene in and out of the Church that will help you better understand what we need to overcome in order to really influence the world the way we are meant to.

Obstacle #1 – Sin and Worldliness

Have you ever considered that sin might stunt your creativity? Do you realize what is happening in the creative realm today? In a presentation about the power of music to influence thoughts, President Boyd K. Packer illustrated the subtle and powerful change happening in the world right now as to what it will accept in its entertainment:

> *...much of the music being performed by popular entertainers today seems to be more intended to agitate than to pacify, more to excite than to calm. Some musicians appear to openly promote unrighteous thoughts and action...How tolerant we have become, and how quickly we are moving.*

He then went on to describe how this same trend has infiltrated virtually every form of entertainment and news source:

> *A generation ago writers of newspapers, editors of magazines, and particularly the producers of motion pictures carefully censored profane and obscene words. Carefully (we are always led carefully), profanity has inched and nudged and pushed its way relentlessly into the motion picture and the magazine, and now even newspapers print verbatim comments, the likes of which would have been considered intolerable a generation ago.*[1]

What does this have to do with us as Artist-Disciples? As Elder Maxwell said, "...sin is the only real tragedy."[2] Sin is a tragedy because it keeps us from "do[ing] the things that [we] would."[3] In other words, sin keeps us from achieving our potential and fulfilling our purpose. Sin literally stops us from having the influence we could have.

Are you being original?

How does sin stop your influence? For starters, consider this: Artists are constantly on the search for new, fresh and different. They want to be leading the latest trend, not left in the dust of other artists. However, sin causes art and creation to be more and more homogenous, not fresh or different. There are only so many ways to use profanity and immorality to entice the natural man. Sin is same-ish. After a while it makes everything look and feel the same. It has no dynamics. Its color spectrum is limited, and when you are trapped by sin, so is your ability to see the vivid palette of expression life offers.

Righteousness, on the other hand, has unlimited creative possibilities. Look at this earth. Even though it is currently telestial and fallen, we can't even describe some of the beauty we experience here. If the earth were created by sin there wouldn't be anywhere near the beauty and color and dynamics we see here on a daily basis. It would be monotone. I believe the only way for Artist-Disciples to be truly unique is to be more righteous. Nothing will set our creative work apart more than righteousness and all its associated ingredients.

Which master are you serving?

One of our greatest challenges as Artist Disciples seeking our uniqueness is trying to find a middle ground between the world's way and who we truly are. The scriptures describe it thus:

> *…every city or house divided against itself shall not stand:*[4]
>
> *No man can serve two masters; for either he will hate the one and love the other, or else he will hold to the one and despise the other. Ye cannot serve God and Mammon.*[5]
>
> *A double minded man is unstable in all his ways.*[6]

How long halt ye between two opinions?[7]

Being divided, serving two masters, being double-minded—all cause our progress to halt. We do not become what we could be if we would just commit, either to the Lord's way or, I hesitate to say, to the world's way. We do not do full justice to either one, and therefore come across to our audiences as, well, uncommitted. Elder Jeffrey R. Holland once spoke about checking our religion at the door.[8] Do we sometimes keep one foot in Zion and one foot in Babylon, checking our sins at the door of the chapel and then checking our religion at the door of the studio or stage? Too often we see the evil in the world, but fear to truly live up to the wholeness of what the Lord offers.

I believe the Lord wants us to be either hot or cold, not lukewarm.[9] As one writer put it, "Some people aren't going to 'get you' or like you or agree with you. And that's ok, because the more YOU you can be, the more you will draw to you the exact people who are resonating completely with you and your message. That's what goes viral."[10] As Artist-Disciples, we become more "us" as we remember and act according to our true identity and by committing wholeheartedly to the Lord. According to Elder Maxwell, "the essence of the gospel of Jesus Christ is that we must clearly choose some things and reject others. Mortal philosophies can be mixed and merged with each other almost at will, because they are not totally dissimilar, but we can't weld the Lord's way to the world's ways."[11]

What does it mean to choose the Lord's way?

Elder Robert D. Hales taught, "As Latter-day Saints we need not look like the world. We need not entertain like the world. Our personal habits should be different. Our recreation should be different."[12] This is not to say that we lock ourselves up in the temple and isolate ourselves from the world. Again, Elder Maxwell teaches,

> *When we speak of letting go of the world, this does not mean forgoing its sunsets, its beautiful music, nor, best of all, its people. The "world" is a way of life that takes us away from, not toward, God. Away from, not toward, happiness. Away from sense to nonsense.*[13]

In other words, as Artist-Disciples, choosing the Lord's way is a combined effort of letting go of the nonsense of the world and accepting all the beautiful and wonderful things it has to offer. Alan Bloom observed, "It may well be that a society's greatest madness seems normal to itself."[4] With the benefits of the gospel of Jesus Christ, Artist-Disciples can recognize the madness for what it is. George Q. Cannon taught,

> *If the breach is daily widening between ourselves and the world…then we may be assured that our progress is certain, however slow. On the opposite hand, if our feelings and affections, our appetites and desires, are in unison with the world around us…we should do well to examine ourselves."*[14]

As our feelings, appetites, affections and desires align more with the Lord, you and I will be given more creative power than we are now experiencing. Our personal righteousness will become the key to unlocking our potential and creating things that have never before been created. God is the author of creation. Satan can only imitate, and his creations are monotone because they are only forms of rebellion from the Creator.

The pull of the world is constant. The current of mainstream art and media is strong. The great and spacious building is deceptive and appealing, but we don't have to go to it or give in to its demands. We can and must remain different from the world so that we can make a difference in the world. If the tug and pull of Babylon seems at times to test your faith and strength beyond your capacity, remember this, "It will take no faith to renounce worldly things when these are among the ashes of a melted planet."[15] No matter how hard the pull of the world is, the Lord's ways are eternal, and they will triumph in the end.

Now is the time to commit, once and for all, to what you are going to stand for with your life and your art.

Obstacle #2 – Isolation

Obviously, Artist-Disciples want to avoid the potential threats of sin and worldliness if we are going to help fulfill the gospel vision of the arts. But is that the only challenge? What else could stop us from achieving what we are here to do?

A Jig and a Light...

I have a talented young friend named Jason who had a deep desire to share the gospel at school. However, because he didn't feel like he "fit in," he isolated himself from people other than his Church friends, limiting his opportunity to share the gospel. Even though he'd been praying for missionary moments, he wasn't having them.

One Sunday he mentioned this frustration to me. Knowing his creative gifts, I encouraged Jason to put himself out there a little bit more. I was surprised when just a few days later he reported to me that he had started a dance trend in one of his classes. Somehow his teacher had observed a "little jig" that Jason did and liked it so much that he asked him to perform in front of the whole class. The class now refers to this dance by Jason's last name. This has led to new friendships and opportunities to talk about the Church. By putting himself out there a little bit, using his creative gifts, and being a leader, this young man opened up doors to make a difference in more people's lives.

Sometimes being an Artist-Disciple is like that. The Lord has instructed us to "Let [our] light so shine before men, that they may see [our] good works, and glorify [our] Father which is in heaven".[16] One of the things that keeps us from achieving our mission and fulfilling the gospel vision of the arts is isolation. Elder Ballard taught,

> *In the Church, we often state the couplet, "Be in the world but not of the world." As we observe television shows that make profanity, violence, and infidelity commonplace and even glamorous, we often wish we could lock out the world in some way and isolate our families from it all...*
>
> *Perhaps we should state the couplet previously mentioned as two separate admonitions. First, "Be in the world." Be involved; be informed. Try to be understanding and tolerant and to appreciate diversity. Make meaningful contributions to society through service and involvement. Second, "Be not of the world." Do not follow wrong paths or bend to accommodate or accept what is not right...*
>
> *Members of the Church need to influence more than we are influenced. We should work to stem the tide of sin and evil instead of passively being swept along by it. We each need to help solve the problem rather than avoid or ignore it.*[17]

Zion is to "be an ensign unto the people, and there shall come unto her out of every nation under heaven."[18] John Taylor said that Zion would become the praise of the whole earth so that kings and rulers would hear of her fame and gaze upon her glory. Clearly, our light was meant to be experienced and seen by the world, not just ourselves.

Who is your audience?

There is an entire market dedicated to LDS art, and this is good and useful. It will only continue to grow in size and excellence. LDS art is needed to strengthen us internally and many of the artists currently operating here will make significant marks in other places as well. We are entering a time when more and more LDS artists must "sally forth"[19] into the world market so that their creative work can be experienced by audiences of all backgrounds.

Elder Maxwell taught the youth of the Church:

> *My beloved young friends, you are the vanguard of the righteous spirit to be infused into the Church in the last days...you were prepared—before the foundations of the world—to help save others in the latter-day world. You cannot keep that resplendent rendezvous if you become like the world! Make your righteous marks on the world instead of being spotted by the world.*[20]

Being the Vanguard

A vanguard is defined as "the troops moving at the head of an army; the forefront of an action or movement."[21] We are not supposed to be waiting back at camp while others fight the battle for us. We should be active in combating evil. As long as we keep ourselves isolated or hold back or put our light under a bushel, we will be limited in the difference we can make.

We came to this earth to change the world, not to let it change us. Do we as Artist-Disciples too often forget the artist part and not seek to change the world? Do we forget the disciple part and let the world change us?

The Lord has charged us to "Arise and shine forth, that [our] light[s] may be a standard for the nations"[22] This true and living Church is coming forth out of obscurity and out of darkness.[23] Will it not become a standard for the nations much more quickly if we decide to arise and shine forth and come out of obscurity and darkness ourselves?

Obstacle #3 – Mediocrity

Why would someone want to listen to, watch, touch, or experience your creative work? Brigham Young invited us to:

> *Learn everything that the children of men know, and be prepared for the most refined society upon the face of the earth. Then improve on this until we are prepared and permitted to enter the society of the blessed— the holy angels, that dwell in the presence of God…*[24]

The third obstacle to achieving our mission and fulfilling the gospel vision of the arts is mediocrity. We can overcome sin and worldliness and we can come out of isolation, but if our creative work is mediocre it's not likely to cut through the secular smog and make the difference it was meant to make. The diagram below demonstrates this obstacle:

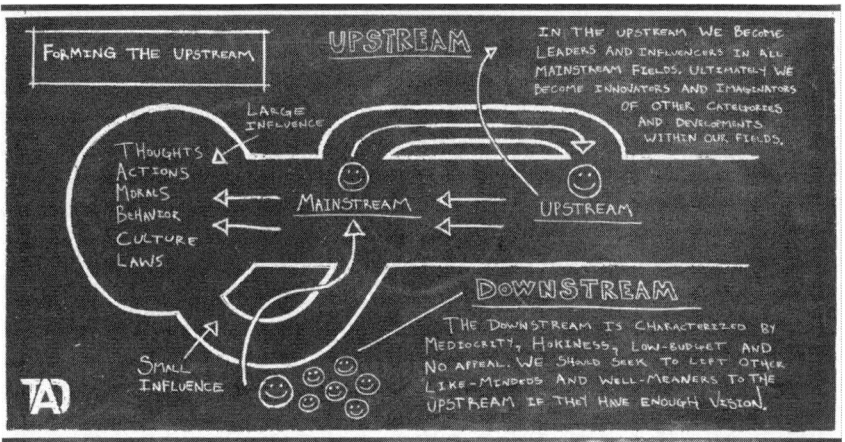

Where are you swimming?

Shown here is a river with a pool at the end. As you can see, the pool represents the thoughts, actions, morals, behavior, culture and laws of society.

There is a small inlet on the bottom side of the pool being fed by the *Downstream*. The Downstream represents art and artists which are well-meaning but mediocre, wholesome but hokey, clean but not appealing. Creations produced by the Downstream tend to be perceived as cheesy, low-budget, low-quality, B-level, and certainly not at the level of excellence one would expect to be mainstream. The Downstream has small influence on the culture and laws of society. It doesn't attract enough attention. In addition, it actually hurts wholesome artistic expression because it makes it seem like "edginess" and appeal are only to be found in sin.

The *Mainstream,* on the other hand, is the primary influencer of the culture and laws of society. The Mainstream is characterized by terms like excellent, high-budget, cool, A-level, 5-star, world-class, high-quality, etc.

In the Mainstream you will find a high level of excellence, a lot of money and resources, strategy, skill, dedication and appeal. You'll also often find a high level of immorality and a low level of standards. However, the Mainstream is where the big fish play. It's where the biggest difference can be made. To stay in the Downstream and hope to make a big difference on society is kind of like digging a hole 50 feet away from the Mississippi River and hoping the river will go out of its way to fill your hole with water. That would be foolish. In order to get some water, you have to get in the current. But beware, the current of the Mainstream is strong and will pull you under if you don't have a strong foundation. The Mainstream is where sin and worldliness, Obstacle #1, lives.

The *Upstream* is a current (no pun intended) idea that is becoming a reality, and the goal and focus of this book. In order to form the

Upstream, Artist-Disciples from the Downstream and Artist-Disciples who are now in the Mainstream overcome Obstacle #2 by coming out of isolation. They "learn everything that the children of men know" and apply it to Upstream principles, avoiding the mediocrity which is Obstacle #3. They pass through the Mainstream without getting pulled in. Then they stand strong in the new Upstream and invite others, both artists and fans, to join them.

Ultimately, the destiny of the Upstream is to become the influencer of the Mainstream and of the culture and laws of society. Those of us who form the Upstream will become the innovators and trendsetters in our fields, creating things that have never been created. We will fulfill the gospel vision of the arts and have a profound influence on the culture and laws of society.

Heading Upstream

Do we understand the power of this idea? My family and I have been so inspired by it that we've given our parent entertainment and media company the name, Upstream International, Inc., so that we keep this stretching ideal in our view constantly. As an Artist-Disciple, the Mainstream is not and should not be our ultimate goal. If it is, then we will fail. It will lead to what I call the great Hollywood Compromise—compromising our standards and selling our birthright to the morals and values of Hollywood, and in so doing, we and the world lose what we are on earth to share. Traveling through the Mainstream is a means, not an end. Its primary purpose is to help us develop the skills and knowledge necessary to overcome the world. As we travel through the Mainstream with the ultimate goal of forming the Upstream, we will be able to process all of the secular learning properly. We will learn how to sell out theaters and shelves without "selling out."

Again, Elder Maxwell eloquently teaches the importance of acquiring secular knowledge:

> *Yes, being learned is good. It can supply us with the needed facts and develop a facility with facts and discernment among facts. It can help us to use our minds to cultivate an intellectual adroitness in connecting the patches of truth and insight. It certainly furthers the calisthenics of the intellect. Finally, however, you and I should be fully qualified and certified in traditional education and its processes for yet another good reason—bilinguality. The men and women of Christ should be truly educated, articulate as to secular knowledge, but should also be educated and articulate in the things of the Spirit."*[25]

In order to make a difference in the world, we must be bilingual; we must speak the language of the world and the language of heaven. The Savior taught his disciples, "Behold, I send you forth as a sheep in the midst of wolves: be ye therefore wise as serpents, and harmless as doves.[26] We, too, can be innocent as to sin, but not naïve to the things of the world. In this process of forming the Upstream and fulfilling the gospel vision of the arts, we can take comfort in knowing that because the Savior has overcome the world, we can overcome it, too.[27]

Now is the Time

How important is the Upstream?

To answer this question, consider the importance of the thoughts, actions, morals, behavior, culture, and laws of society. The Upstream has a direct effect on each of these areas. To a large degree, it will direct your life, and the lives of your children and grandchildren.

What you and I create today becomes the world in which we are swimming in tomorrow. And how far our creations reach may determine the course which our nation and civilization pursue for generations.

We have no time to waste. It's time we get out of the Downstream. It's time we overcome the temptations of the Mainstream. It's time we defeat the Three Obstacles.

How do we do this? Enter *Forming the Upstream*.

Questions and Action Items:

1. Who do you want to become? Make a list of the qualities you would like to have and dreams you want to pursue. How does the art and media you choose on a daily basis affect these goals? Does it lead you toward or away from reaching them? What adjustments need to be made?

2. Which of the Obstacles is the biggest challenge for you? How are you working to overcome it?

3. What are your hesitations for sharing your offering? Do you have a habit that, once released, would supercharge your influence for good?

4. How can you speak the languages of heaven and earth, while still having Christ as your center?

Chapter Summary

- There are three primary challenges that keep Artist-Disciples from having the kind of powerful impact they could have. These Three Obstacles are:
    - Obstacle #1 – Sin and Worldliness
    - Obstacle #2 – Isolation

- - -
    - o   Obstacle #3 - Mediocrity
  - As Artist-Disciples overcome the Three Obstacles and implement the other techniques and truths taught in this book, they will come out of the Downstream, overcome the Mainstream and form a new Upstream.
  - The Upstream is the place where the gospel vision of the arts is fulfilled. Artist-Disciples who form the Upstream will have significant and positive impact on the culture, laws and values of society.

---

[1] Boyd K. Packer, "The Message: Worthy Music, Worthy Thoughts," *New Era*, April 2008.
[2] Neal A. Maxwell, "Shine as Lights in the World," *Ensign*, May 1983.
[3] Galatians 5:16-17.
[4] Matthew 12:25.
[5] 3 Nephi 13:24.
[6] James 1:8.
[7] 1 Kings 18:21.
[8] Jeffrey R. Holland, "Israel, Israel, God is Calling," CES Devotional, 2012.
[9] Revelation 3:16.
[10] Marnie Pehrson, marniepehrson.com/unplugged/2013/02/21/getting-your-tribe-to-market-for-you/.
[11] Neal A. Maxwell, *The Neal A. Maxwell Quote Book*, 422.
[12] Robert D. Hales, as quoted by Larry W. Gibbons, "Wherefore, Settle This in Your Hearts," *Ensign*, November 2006.
[13] Maxwell, *The Neal A. Maxwell Quote Book*, 423.
[14] George Q. Cannon, *Aaronic Priesthood Manual 2*, 160.
[15] Maxwell, *The Neal A. Maxwell Quote Book*, 424.
[16] Matthew 5:16.
[17] M. Russell Ballard, as quoted by The Church of Jesus Christ of Latter-day Saints, *Old Testament Gospel Doctrine Teacher's Manual*, 35.
[18] Doctrine and Covenants 64:42.
[19] 3 Nephi 4:1.
[20] Maxwell, *The Neal A. Maxwell Quote Book*, 422.
[21] Merriam-Webster Online Dictionary, merriam-webster.com/dictionary/vanguard.
[22] Doctrine and Covenants 115:5.
[23] Doctrine and Covenants 1:30.

[24] Brigham Young, as quoted by Spencer W. Kimball, "The Gospel Vision of the Arts," *Ensign,* July 1977.
[25] Neal A. Maxwell, "The Inexhaustible Gospel," BYU Devotional, August 18, 1992.
[26] Matthew 10:16.
[27] John 16:33; 1 John 5:4; Doctrine and Covenants 63:47.

Section II: Forming the Upstream

Lesson 4:
The Foundation

Artist-Disciple Insights

Kristina's Story: Part of Who He Was

It was at a musical fireside that I learned a lesson about discipleship that would forever change the way I think about performing. I was on the program to play one of my favorite pieces. I love it because it brings the Spirit and the people in the audience would always come up afterwards and say they felt it and appreciated my playing.

Even though I perform every day professionally and had played that piece quite a few times before, I still got nervous because I wanted to present it as well as I possibly could. I really wanted to pay tribute to the beautiful music through a flawless performance. When I finished I smiled because I felt we performed excellently.

The next musical number was a guy in our ward I knew pretty well, and not only did I know him, but I knew he could sing! I was excited to hear his beautiful rendition of "Jesus, Savior, Pilot Me." He sang it flawlessly through the first two verses. What happened next, though, changed my heart. As he started singing the words, "When at last I near the shore, and the fearful breakers roar," his voice was strong, but when he started singing about reaching the Savior and what Christ would say to him, tears filled his eyes, and mine, and the rest of the congregation's, as well.

He tried to sing the last part of the song, but it came out almost as if it was just spoken because he was so overcome by the love he felt for Christ. I was shocked. Not because he cried, but because he felt it so much that whether he sang or spoke the words, it didn't matter. I KNEW through his performance that he LOVED his Savior. I knew it.

After he got down, I sat there with tears now running down my face because I was fervently repenting. I was ashamed that I had thought so much about how I would do rather than what I was playing about and what it meant to me.much about how I would do rather than what I was playing about and what it meant to me.

I don't believe it's a sin to care about doing well, but it is to forget the reason why you do it. In my self-consciousness, I had lost sight of my reasons for performing.

Because of this man's example, I now want everyone within my reach to know I love Him. He didn't have to act or put on a face of spirituality. Those lyrics were a part of who he was.

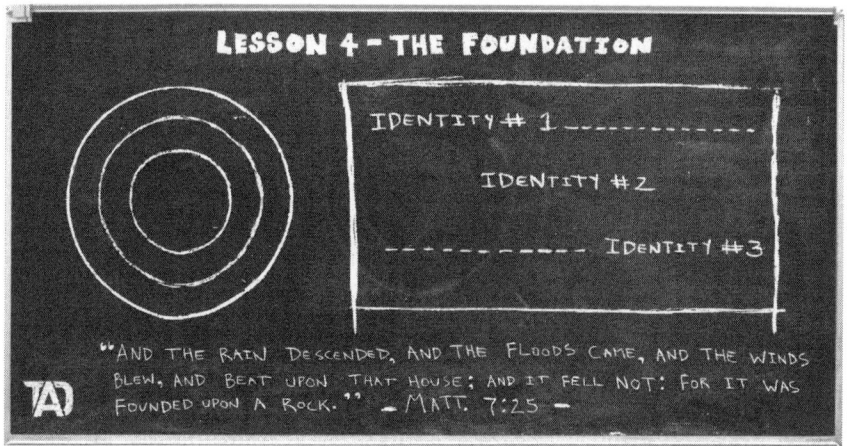

How do we form the Upstream?

If you are anything like me, your next question after understanding our potential as Artist-Disciples and what may have stopped us in the past is, "Then how do we really do it?"

To truly change our lives and the future of the world through the arts, we need to make sure we are solidly founded in truth. That is why this lesson is called "The Foundation." It is a starting place to ensure everything else works. Because the current of the mainstream is so strong and because the pull of the Three Obstacles is so powerful, we need to understand some key things about who we really are and what we are really here to do in order to overcome them and form the Upstream. Although we have touched on some of these concepts earlier, it is important to fully integrate them now. This lesson is all about building a strong foundation based on Three Identities and Three Rings.

Three Identities

Each of us has three identities, three aspects of who we are which affect our ability to create. A solid understanding of these identities is the first piece in the foundation of Artist-Discipleship.

First Identity: Child of God

What is your place in the world?

Chances are the answer to this question is also directly connected to how you view your life and your art. Your perception of who you are is like a pair of glasses that affects your interpretation and explanation of everything else.

As a full-time missionary in Portland, Oregon, my companion and I would start our lessons with the hymn, "I Am a Child of God." As we sang the words of that hymn with our investigators, this essential truth—that we are literally spirit children of a loving Heavenly Father—touched our hearts and often brought us and our investigators to tears. There's a reason missionaries start the teaching process with this simple and fundamental principle.

Know Yourself

Both Joseph Smith and Brigham Young said: "No man ... can know himself unless he knows God, and he cannot know God unless he knows himself."[1] Truly, as Elder Dallin H. Oaks observed, "We must begin with the truth about God and our relationship to him. Everything else follows from that."[2]

Think about it. You and I and every other person we ever meet are literally children of the most powerful Being in the Universe. If we keep this identity in view constantly, we will consistently stay on course. In fact, our knowledge of who we are should inform all of our daily and life decisions.

So, why does this matter to the Artist-Disciple? First of all, as one of my fellow Artist-Disciple friends, Diane, once put it: "Everyone you talk to is more important than the chair you're sitting on." Our life as an Artist-Disciple is about service to mankind. We will be more to serve when we understand the immense possibilities of we are serving.

Secondly, understanding our own immense possibilities as a child of God will help us to reach higher artistically, to conquer obstacles when they come, and to become everything we are capable of becoming.

In short, understanding and embracing our identity as children of God gives us the right view of the world. Without this fundamental knowledge, our foundation will be faulty, which will make our walls and roofs faulty as well. This one mistake will ensure that a thousand mistakes follow.

On the other hand, if we let this truth sink into our hearts and into our decisions, then our choices will be directed optimally, and many mistakes will be limited or avoided altogether—artistically, personally, eternally. As we choose to embrace the First Identity fully, everything else in our lives will shift. As our lives change, our art and the world around us will begin to shift as well.

Second Identity: Artist

Children do it naturally, from mud pies to crayon illustrations; from chords on the piano and stories they make up to share. Inherently, they are expressing aspects of our Second Identity, which has to do with the characteristics we share as children of a creative God, made in His image. God is the creator of worlds without number.[3] As His children we have inherited, in embryo, His creative nature. This is important to understand, especially for this book. As I mentioned earlier, some people don't consider themselves to be creative or artistic. But we all are—by nature—creators.

President Dieter F. Uchtdorf spoke to this point in an address given at the General Relief Society meeting of the October 2008 General Conference:

> *The desire to create is one of the deepest yearnings of the human soul. No matter our talents, education, backgrounds, or abilities, we each have an inherent wish to create something that did not exist before…Everyone can create…Creation brings deep satisfaction and fulfillment…Remember that you are spirit daughters [and sons] of the most creative Being in the universe. Isn't it remarkable to think that your very spirits are fashioned by an endlessly creative and eternally compassionate God?*[4]

Isn't it remarkable to think about? Can you feel the truth of President Uchtdorf's words in your own life? When was the last time you planted a seed, tidied a room, or sang a song? Whatever it is you are creating, what inspires you to do it? If you have a notebook or another device handy, take a moment and jot down some of your answers to these questions.

Why create?

As I mentioned in the Introduction, I teach *The Artist Disciple* (TAD) courses to Artist-Disciples from all over the world. I am always fascinated in their answers to the question "What motivates you to engage in your creative work?" Here are some of their responses:

> *"Just a feeling that I have in my heart…"* – Andrea

> *"My passion for it…"* – Esita

> *"The Holy Ghost…"* – Kathryn

> *"Something that is difficult to put into words… it's more of a feeling deeply ingrained in my heart."* – Briahna

"A desire to bless others. A desire to fulfill my life mission and develop the talents God has given me..." – John

"The joy of holding my children and looking into their precious eyes. The joy of meeting people who have partaken of my service or musical talents and been changed or influenced in some positive way..." – Renee

"I know the desire to create is a God-given desire and I want to use everything He's given me to please Him." – Josh

"I don't know what my engine is, to be honest. Something drives me forward, and if I try to be mediocre, every aspect of my life deteriorates—and the only way I can feel happy, is in doing very bold activities. It is like God says, 'No, that isn't good enough, I want you to do something greater—you were meant for something greater.' So I personally believe that God is what motivates me to engage in my creative work." – Saul

These responses and yours confirm what President Uchtdorf said—that we each have an "inherent" desire to create. I want to suggest to you that what motivates you to engage in creative work is your nature. It is who you are. It's part of your spiritual and physical DNA. It's the Lord, the Light of Christ, and the Holy Ghost *outside* of you, and it's your nature *inside* of you. You can't get rid of your divine nature, so let's do something with it. Let's channel it in a positive, Kingdom-building direction. Subway has "sandwich artists." The Lord needs "Kingdom artists." He needs people who will be co-creators with Him in bringing about His great and eternal work. Every one of us, no matter how artistic we believe we are, is a creator in the sense that we are composing our individual lives—each small brush stroke on "the canvas of [our] souls"[5] contributing to what will eventually be the masterpiece of our character. That is true artistry.

Whether we realize it or not, each one of us is in the process of creation every day, and our works of art can and do have far-reaching effects on our perspective, relationships, and personal influence. It is my hope that our discussion in this book so far has helped and will continue to help you discover and fully embrace this identity, and use it to be the most spectacular "Kingdom artist" you can be for the blessing of the world.

Third Identity: Disciple

This Identity is mentioned third because it is more a chosen identity than an inherited identity like the first two are. It is more nurture than nature. Before we came to this earth, we all chose to follow Christ in the pre-mortal war in heaven.[6] Thus we kept our first estate. In order to keep our second estate, we must choose to follow Christ again.[7] Those who choose to follow Christ again in this second estate become His disciples.

Have you ever considered yourself to be a disciple? What does this word mean to you? Until picking up this book, you might have never thought of yourself as a disciple before, referring to yourself as a Latter-day Saint, or a Christian, or a "member," reserving the special title of disciple for the Twelve or for those with more position or apparent spiritual prominence in the Church. However, the Bible Dictionary defines "disciple" thusly: "A pupil or learner; a name used to denote (1) the twelve, also called apostles, (2) *all* followers of Jesus Christ."[8] So "all followers of Jesus Christ" are disciples. Do you consider yourself a follower of Jesus Christ?

Trying to Be Like Jesus

Those of us who have decided to follow the Master are His disciples. We, like Him, are about our Father's business which, as Elder Maxwell once observed, is really being about the business of trying to be more like Jesus.[9] The reality is that by choosing to be members of Christ's Church, we have chosen to be His disciples. We should proudly accept this title and respond to what it means. Doing so is essential for our spiritual growth and it enhances all of our creative pursuits.

In practical terms, being a disciple could mean loving as He loves, acting as He acts, creating as He creates. Being a disciple is a choice we make to align our thoughts and wills and intents with the Master. It means we go to *Him* to be taught, and we go to *Him* to be inspired, and we go to *Him* for feedback and approval of our work. Being a disciple of Christ is a daily, ongoing choice that yields greater and greater rewards the more we choose to embrace it.

Three Identities Summary – Checks and Balances

What is the power of knowing our Three Identities? When we acknowledge that we are children of God, choose to be disciples of Christ, and allow these two identities to inform all of our decisions, then our Second Identity, that of being an Artist, takes its proper place—sandwiched between the other two. If we are to build the Kingdom as we can and must, our Second Identity—our creative and artistic nature—should always be framed or book-ended by our First Identity and our Third Identity. These act as guard rails to keep our Second Identity on the straight and narrow. Without these guardrails, it becomes easy for us to fall into one of the Three Obstacles.

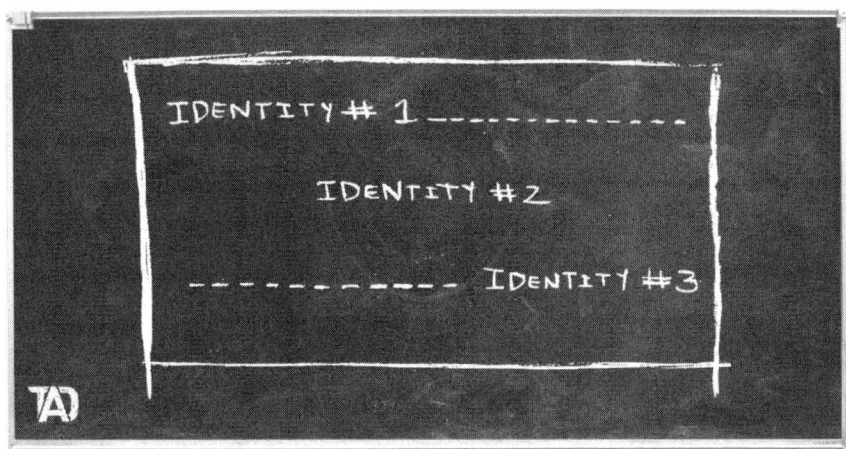

Slavery v. Freedom

Earlier, we discussed this statement from the Prophet Joseph Smith: "…Man of himself is an instrument of music and…whether the music is produced by the human voice or an instrument, it arrests his attention and absorbs his whole being."[10] All artistic pursuits, not just music, have this tendency and power—to arrest our attention and absorb our whole being. Whether you are a computer programmer or a concrete sculptor, and whether you are climbing the career ladder or the music charts, we all need to be careful to ensure that our Second Identity doesn't consume us.

On the other hand, Jesus taught that the truth shall make us free.[11] It certainly will. The best art is created within the bounds of truth in our eternal nature and by the integrity of our chosen discipleship. Without boundaries, good and lasting art really doesn't happen. Our First and Third Identities act as guardrails—as a check and balance system for our Second Identity. Within these boundaries, our Second Identity will eventually soar.

Three Rings

You have heard it before:

"Follow your bliss."

"Do what you love and the money will follow."

"Find your purpose and live it."

"Do what you were born to do."

And *"What do you want to be when you grow up?"*

As an artistic and creative person, you probably ask "What am I born to do?" often. Pop psychology, religion, talk shows, and self-help literature repeat the mantra about finding your purpose, your calling, your mission, and living your passion.

While the advice to "go for it" is plentiful, *how* to actually go about it is not. Fortunately, with our Three Identities firmly in place, we are ready to expand and lay the next part of our foundation. We now move from Three Identities to Three Rings.

A Life at the Circus...

As I've studied, prayed, pondered, fasted and sought to live the Lord's will for me, I've come to the conclusion that life is a three-ring circus. A three-ring circus is defined as "a circus having simultaneous performances in three separate rings."[12] The world often defines a three-ring circus as a chaotic set of circumstances where nothing seems to fit together or be in balance. God is a God of order[13]—so why are we talking about three-ring circuses? In the Lord's three ring's circus, each of the rings is interrelated and works in synergy with the others. Here's a picture of what I have learned about God's three-ring circus—the parts of our purpose and calling and how they are truly related. Let's start filling in the blanks.

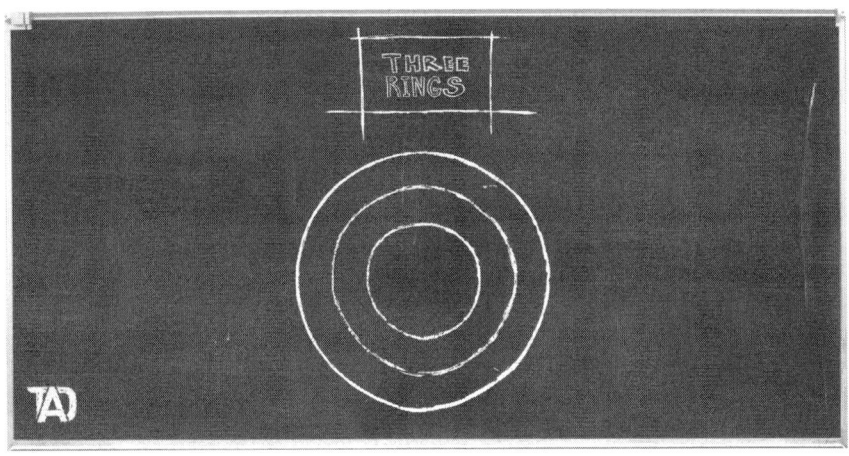

Three Rings – Ring #1: Purpose

Have you ever struggled to discover your most important priority, what it is and what it should be?

For many years I struggled with this question. I was hesitant to move forward in my life as an artist—or as an anything—unless I was confident my life was matching up with the Lord's purposes for it. Of all the gospel principles, practices, policies, programs, people, and ideas, which was the most important for me to center on? What was the one sure thing I could always focus on, an "organizing principle"[14] around which everything else could fit? I knew in my spirit that there was such a thing, but I couldn't seem to find it. What was my purpose as Brydon Brett?

Can you relate? Have you ever felt like life offers so many paths leading to many good places, but what you want is the best place? Have you ever wondered how to discover your most essential purpose? I mean, are we here to have families? Are we in this for happiness? Is it about charity? Are we here to keep the commandments? Is our purpose to prove ourselves? Are we meant to be perfect, even as our Father and Savior are perfect? Does it feel like there is too much to think about all at once?

Of course, you know as I knew that the answer to all of these questions (except, perhaps, for the last one) is YES. As children of God, we are to focus on, do, and become all of these things. But for me, there had to be a way to express or think about all of this without becoming over-focused on one practice or principle, something that coordinates all of these eternal objectives.

Spiritually, I knew there was such an organizing principle, but it was elusive to me.

Something was missing.

Becoming as He is

Toward the end of my mission, I vividly recall being frustrated and unsatisfied with all the work I had *done*. Honestly, my companions and I had broken mission records, I had served in every leadership position possible, and by all accounts had enjoyed a decorated and honorable full-time mission. But I felt empty. It was during a rainy morning study while I was in the middle of this emptiness that I was led to a thought that completely changed my paradigm and my life:

> *Some chapters in "Preach My Gospel" focus on what you need to do as a missionary— how to study, how to teach, how to manage time wisely. Just as vital as what you do, however, is who you are. The restored gospel enables you to become like Heavenly Father and Jesus Christ. The Savior has shown the way. He has set the perfect example, and He commands us to become as He is (see 3 Nep. 27:27). Learn of Him and seek to incorporate His attributes into your life. Through the power of His Atonement, you can achieve this goal and lead others to achieve it also.*[15]

This might be old news to you, but for me it probably constitutes the most impacting truth I've ever learned by the Spirit. It was a capstone truth that coordinated all of my questions and put them into one umbrella answer. I'd always heard this, but I'd never really *heard* it. Finally, on that rainy Portland morning, this truth made the long journey from my head to my heart and I understood by the Spirit that **my purpose is to *become* like Heavenly Father and Jesus Christ.**

Not just do. Become.

Everything in the gospel is intended to help me fulfill this purpose. This truth can become the coordinating, organizing principle of my life as a disciple—and yours. If we apply it, it brings life, energy and excitement to every second of every day.

Noted speaker and author Miles Monroe once said, "If purpose is unknown, abuse is inevitable."[16] In other words, if we don't know what our reasons are for doing and acting a certain way, we will inevitably get off course. If purpose is known, however, then righteous results are inevitable. Our purpose is the litmus test for everything we do. If a behavior or decision does not contribute to becoming like Christ and building up the Kingdom of God, then we need to question whether it is worth our time. Of course, knowing, doing, and being are all part of this process and there is much more to it. In the end, our purpose is to become like our Heavenly Father and Jesus Christ.

Three Rings – Ring #2: Calling(s)

Okay, so we've discussed our fundamental purpose for being on this earth. I hope that truth really sinks in for you. It can make all the difference in your life if it does. Once purpose is firmly in place in your mind, your heart, and your lifestyle, then your other rings start to come into focus as well.

Let's talk about Ring #2. Popular jargon in the world today likes to refer to your life's work—that thing which you are "meant" to do—as your calling. Typically they are referring to a professional pursuit, a lifelong project, or a career choice. I only mention this because that is *not* how we will refer to it in this class. What the rest of the world means by "calling," I refer to as "mission" or "offering," which we will discuss in Ring #3. So what do *I* mean by calling(s)? As I define it, we have two types of callings in this life:

- First, eternal roles and responsibilities (e.g., father, mother, husband, wife, etc.).
- Second, priesthood callings and assignments (e.g., bishop, Relief Society president, full-time missionary, etc.).

What is central?

In *The Family: A Proclamation to the World,* the First Presidency and Council of the Twelve state that "…marriage between a man and a woman is ordained of God and that *the family is central* to the Creator's plan for the eternal destiny of His children."[17]

There is no better environment for developing Christlike attributes than in the home. As President David O. McKay said, "No other success can compensate for failure in the home," and because of this truth, high priority needs to be placed on the family. Furthermore, of all the roles and responsibilities we have or will have in this life, our familial roles are the only ones we know for sure we will take with us into the eternities.[18] Simply put, family comes before the Church. The Church exists to help and strengthen families.

Of all your possible endeavors as a creator and an artist, creating an eternal family as a parent, sibling, and child is the most important. Family is where creative work begins. Family is where creative work continues. Family is the reason for creation. If we miss out on family, it really doesn't matter where our other creative endeavors take us. Whatever your family situation, now would be a good time to pull out your journal and jot down some ideas of how you can show devotion to your family, and how they are central to all your other work.

Kingdom First

In addition to our eternal family roles and responsibilities, our priesthood callings and assignments are also found in Ring #2. While they are not to supplant our eternal family roles and responsibilities, they are still vitally important to our happiness and exaltation because they have a direct effect on the building up of the Kingdom of God. We have covenanted to fulfill them—both pre-mortally and mortally.

The Prophet Joseph Smith said, "Every man who has a calling to minister to the inhabitants of the world was ordained to that very purpose in the Grand Council of heaven before this world was. I suppose I was ordained to this very office in that Grand Council."[19]

You may not be as familiar with this profound statement from President Spencer W. Kimball regarding the foreordination of both men and women to priesthood callings and assignments:

> *Remember, in the world before we came here, faithful women were given certain assignments while faithful men were foreordained to certain priesthood tasks. While we do not now remember the particulars, this does not alter the glorious reality of what we once agreed to. You are accountable for those things which long ago were expected of you just as are those we sustain as prophets and apostles...This leaves much to be done by way of parallel personal development—for both men and women.*[20]

Magnifying our priesthood callings and assignments is part of what we agreed to do before we came to this earth, and it is part of choosing the Kingdom of God first while we are here. Elder Maxwell said, "I testify that what a wise man wrote is true: 'If you have not chosen the Kingdom of God first, it will in the end make no difference what you have chosen instead.'"[21]

Your Most Important Job

Prioritizing Ring #2 over the other things that compete for our time will help us have happiness in this life and eternal life in the world to come.[22] For me, Ring #2 is where I find my greatest joy and my greatest experiences. Is this true for you?

It's in Ring #2 where most of that which matters most happens. It is also in Ring #2 where Ring #1—our purpose—is fulfilled best. Thus we should dedicate great focus and priority to fulfilling our eternal roles and responsibilities as well as our priesthood callings and assignments. As Elder Dallin H. Oaks said, "I have never known of a man who looked back on his working life and said, 'I just didn't spend enough time with my job.'"[23]

Three Rings – Ring #3: Mission or Offering

Art or music, sales or authoring, mothering or mentoring, Ring #3 is your mission or offering. It is the place where the answer to "What am I supposed to do? What am I meant to do? What mission does God want me to perform in this life?" becomes vitally important.

I like to refer to mission as an "offering" for several reasons. Offering implies giving—something you have to *offer* the world. It suggests a leader-servant mentality, that you are giving your offering for the benefit of the world and not for selfish reasons.

I also like the tone of the word "mission." Just like someone who has a mission to complete in a battle zone, it implies that you've been charged with a special task or set of tasks that you are accountable to perform. It suggests urgency and a need to complete it so you can receive other missions.

Because of the layers of meaning associated with these two terms, I will use them interchangeably throughout this book.

What are you here to do?

Do you have a mission to perform?

James Russell Lowell said it this way: "No man is ever born into the world whose work is not born with him. Everyone has a job to be done which he is supposed to do and which he can do better than anyone else in the world."[24]

We know that priesthood callings and assignments are foreordained and that many spiritual leaders were numbered among the noble and great ones pre-mortally[25] and given specific spiritual missions to fulfill. But is the same true of other mortal missions or offerings? Is it true of yours? Bruce R McConkie taught:

> *To carry forward his own purposes among men and nations, the Lord foreordained chosen spirit children in the pre-existence and assigned them to come to earth at particular times and places so that they might aid in furthering the divine will. These pre-existent appointments made "according to the foreknowledge of God the Father" (1 Pet. 1:2), simply designated certain individuals to perform missions which the Lord in his wisdom knew they had the talents and capacities to do.*[26]

Does this mean you? We know that spiritual leaders like Abraham, John the Baptist, Joseph Smith, Mary the mother of Jesus and others were foreordained to their very important spiritual missions before the foundations of the earth. Is it reasonable to believe that great secular leaders like Christopher Columbus, the Founding Fathers, and others were also foreordained? Again, Bruce R. McConkie offers thought-provoking answers:

> *All the spirits of men, while yet in the Eternal Presence, developed aptitudes, talents, capacities, and abilities of every sort, kind, and degree... When we pass from pre-existence to mortality, we bring with us the traits and talents there developed. True, we forget what went before because we are here being tested, but the capacities and abilities that then were ours are yet resident within us. Mozart is still a musician; Einstein retains his mathematical abilities; Michelangelo his artistic talent; Abraham, Moses, and the prophets their spiritual talents and abilities... And all men with their infinitely varied talents and personalities pick up the course of progression where they left it off when they left the heavenly realms.*[27]

So, even if you're not foreordained to be the next president of the Church, you still have a mission. You have something to offer the world. Do you believe this? Are you one of the people who spend a great deal of time trying to figure out your mission?

While there's no time to enumerate all of the principles to finding your life mission, I will say that it takes a lot of work. It is not always easy. It requires seeking diligently and putting forth a lot of effort. It requires wrestling with the Lord, doing your homework, fasting, counseling with leaders and parents, reading your patriarchal blessing and a host of other things; but ultimately it is worth it.

Incredible Journey

When I finally landed on what I felt I was supposed to do, I woke up every morning with purpose and energy. It was exhilarating. I have also found that over time, as you're flexible and receptive, more elements of your personal mission are revealed and the Lord takes you on an incredible journey. He has done so with me. As we put forth the effort to find our mission, we find the joy, energy and satisfaction that come from living life with all three rings in play.

One final word on missions or offerings. The specific nature or application of our individual offerings will differ widely. But even with such diversity, we all share a common mission—to preach repentance. This is important to remember. Your mission might lead you to Hollywood and mine might lead me to Madison Square Garden, but we are all on the same team in helping the world to repent and improve. That is the ultimate aim of the missions the Lord tasks us with—to benefit and better the world and His children.

Three Rings Summary

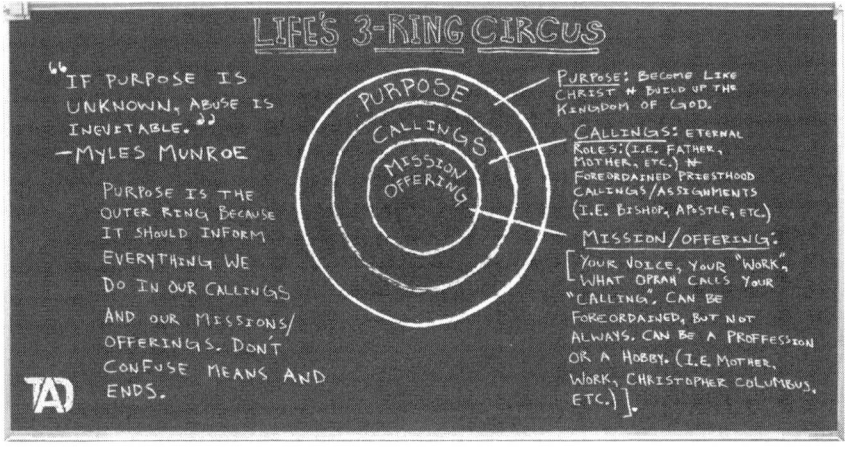

Life is a three-ring circus. Each of us has many roles and responsibilities that happen simultaneously, but unlike the chaos of the world's circuses, the Lord's rings are powerfully synergistic if we perform them well. The Lord has given all of us many opportunities. He has given us Christlike attributes, spiritual gifts, talents and abilities, time and resources. Spiritual gifts are not just reserved for Rings #1 and #2. They can and should be used in Ring #3. Likewise, "secular" gifts can and should be used in all of the Rings. All work synergistically to help us fulfill our purposes within each.

Remember also that Ring #3 wants to supersede Rings #1 and #2. It wants to consume our focus and our time. Making sure we have a solid foundation in Rings #1 and #2 will help to stay grounded and able to fight against the temptation to let Ring #3 get bigger than it should be. With these Three Rings firmly in place, life will be filled with joy and purpose and creativity will soar in the right direction.

Founded

Alright, we just covered a lot of stuff. Take a deep breath. Can you see how the principles and doctrines we've discussed are as wide as eternity and have profound meaning for every area of our lives?

I invite you to review this lesson and your notes on these topics frequently. I know you will find new layers of meaning and understanding each time you do. Because these concepts are so fundamental, we will be returning to and expanding upon them throughout the rest of the book.

Now that we've laid a foundation of understanding with our *Three Identities* and our *Three Rings,* let's continue Upstream...

> ### Questions and Action Items:
>
> 1. Have you seen examples of what happens to well-meaning artists who forget their identities of child of God, and of disciple? What can you do to prevent this in your own life?
>
> 2. What actions are you inspired to take to fulfill your callings, both earthly and eternal?
>
> 3. Do you have a sense of your own mortal mission or offering?
>
> 4. How do you see your unique mission or offering being used to advance His kingdom?

Chapter Summary

- We each share Three Identities as Artist-Disciples and they should inform all of our life and creative decisions. These identities are:
    - First Identity – Child of God
    - Second Identity – Artist
    - Third Identity – Disciple
- We each have Three Rings as Artist-Disciples and these too should inform all of our life and creative decisions. These rings are:
    - Ring #1 – Purpose
    - Ring #2 – Calling(s)
    - Ring #3 – Mission or Offering
- In order to have the kind of foundation necessary to form the Upstream, you will need to be firmly rooted in your Three Identities and your Three Rings.

[1] Joseph Smith, as quoted by Andrew F. Ehat and Lyndon W. Cook, *The Words of Joseph Smith*, 340.
[2] Dallin H. Oaks, "Apostasy and Restoration," *Ensign*, May 1995.
[3] see Moses 1:33; Colossians 1:16.
[4] Dieter F. Uchtdorf, "Happiness, Your Heritage," *Ensign*, November 2008.
[5] David A. Bednar, "More Diligent and Concerned at Home," *Ensign*, November 2009.
[6] Revelation 12:7-11.
[7] Abraham 3:26.
[8] The Church of Jesus Christ of Latter-day Saints, *Bible Dictionary*, 657.
[9] Neal A. Maxwell, "The New Testament—A Matchless Portrait of the Savior," *Ensign*, December 1986.
[10] Joseph Young, *History of the Organization of the Seventies*, 14-15.
[11] John 8:32.
[12] Merriam-Webster Online Dictionary, merriam-webster.com/dictionary/three%20ring%20circus.
[13] Doctrine and Covenants 132:8
[14] Stephen R. Covey, *The Divine Center*, IX.
[15] The Church of Jesus Christ of Latter-day Saints, *Preach my Gospel*, 114.
[16] Miles Monroe, bible.com/notes/2625553/purpose.
[17] Robert D. Hales, "The Eternal Family," *Ensign*, November 1996 (emphasis added).
[18] Doctrine and Covenants 130:2.
[19] Joseph Smith, as quoted by David B. Haight, "Sustaining a New Prophet," Ensign, May 1995.
[20] Spencer W. Kimball, as quoted by Randal Wright, *Achieving Your Life Mission*, 7.
[21] Neal A. Maxwell, "Response to a Call," *Ensign*, May 1974, 112.
[22] Moses 6:59.
[23] Dallin H. Oaks, "Good, Better, Best," *Ensign*, November 2007.
[24] James Russell Lowell, as quoted by Randal Wright, *Achieving Your Life Mission*, 1.
[25] Abraham 3:22-25.
[26] Bruce R. McConkie, *Mormon Doctrine* (2nd Edition), 290.
[27] Bruce R. McConkie, as quoted by The Church of Jesus Christ of Latter-day Saints, *The Gospel and the Productive Life Student Manual Religion 150*, 45.

Lesson 5:
The Lodestar

Artist-Disciple Insights

Paul's Story: Music as an Instrument

My experience came in a tiny pueblo called Zamorano outside the city of Tegucigalpa in Honduras. I was serving as a full-time missionary among the wonderful Honduran people and had been assigned to serve in this little branch where probably about 50 or 60 people came to church each Sunday. I had been out serving for about 5 months and my Spanish was not very good yet, but I knew that the language of the Spirit and the power of music to touch hearts are universal.

I stood to sing "Un Pobre Forastero" (A Poor Wayfaring Man of Grief) with a prayer in my heart, and wondering if my voice singing a capella to a people whose culture was so different from my own would be able connect and touch their hearts. Throughout the hymn I tried to focus on the message of service, of hope, and joy. As I finished and sat down, President Molina, the branch president, stood and with tears in his eyes bore a heartfelt testimony of the truths about which I had just sung. I once again knew that Heavenly Father had used music through me as an instrument to touch the hearts of His children.

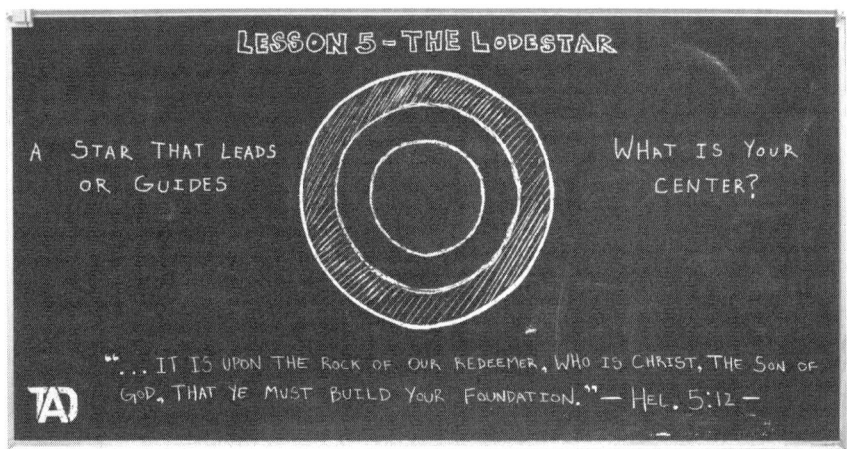

What is a Lodestar?

I once had the opportunity to sit down with a very respected and wise spiritual leader and ask him some questions. I was particularly interested in this leader's opinions about the role music could play in spreading the gospel and how I could make the right career choice in the arts. He shared several insights related to the gospel vision of the arts, and ended with this counsel, "In all your artistic endeavors, Christ must remain the lodestar of your life." He emphasized that he saw so many Church members, artists or not, trying to make the gospel fit their lifestyle. "You need to make your profession fit the Church, not the other way around," he said.[1]

With that, he saw me off and I was left with a lot to ponder. Immediately, I looked up the definition of lodestar on my smartphone. I learned that a lodestar is "a star that leads or guides; one that serves as an inspiration, model, or guide."[2]

Forming the Upstream

In Lesson 4, we discussed our Foundation for building Upstream lives and artists. The Lodestar is a second lesson about what sets the

Upstream apart from its Mainstream counterparts. It builds on the Foundation and goes into depth about where our center is and truly can be. As Artist-Disciples, it is essential that Christ is our leading star.

What would He do?

"What would Jesus do?" The question is so common, both in and out of the Church, that we may sometimes forget how essential it is, and just how big an impact it can have in our lives. Have you had an experience where just remembering what the Savior would do has changed your decision? Have you applied those same principles to your creative endeavors?

I invite you to ponder the following familiar statements with a fresh outlook, and then ask yourself this question: "What role should Christ play in my creative work?"

> *And now, my sons, remember, remember that it is upon the rock of our Redeemer, who is Christ, the son of God, that ye must build your foundation; that when the devil shall send forth his mighty winds, yea, his shafts in the whirlwind, yea, when all his hail and his mighty storm shall beat upon you, it shall have no power over you to drag you down to the gulf of misery and endless wo, because of the rock upon which ye are built, which is a sure foundation, a foundation whereon if men build they cannot fall.* [3]

> *But seek ye first the kingdom of God and his righteousness, and all these things shall be added unto you.* [4]

> *The Kingdom of heaven is first and foremost with us.* [5]

> *Indeed, blessed are those [people] whose lives revolve around the Son.* [6]

When we put God first, all other things fall into their proper place or drop out of our lives. ⁷

Allowing Christ to lead or guide our creation opens us up to the power of heaven. As Christ serves as an inspiration, model, and guide in our creative process, we will know what is important and what is not. We will stay centered on eternal priorities and on what will make the most difference in building up His Kingdom. Our allegiance will be to Him first and not to our own creative instinct. Over time, these creative instincts become more like His.

Where is your center?

The first commandment God gave Moses on Sinai had to do with what we center our lives on. He said, "Thou shalt have no other gods before me. Thou shalt not make unto thee any graven image, or any likeness of anything that is in heaven above, or that is in the earth beneath, or that is in the water under the earth:"⁸ For our purposes, a "center" is the thing around which our lives, decisions, priorities, and self-worth revolve.

The Lord's indictment of idolatry should cause us to inspect what we center our lives on. One definition of idolatry is "immoderate attachment or devotion to something."⁹ When we are immoderately attached or devoted to anything except Christ, we become imbalanced and we lose creative power. President Spencer W. Kimball taught,

> *Idolatry is among the most serious of sins…Modern idols or false gods can take such forms as clothes, homes, businesses, machines, automobiles, pleasure boats, and numerous other material deflectors from the path to godhood…Intangible things make just as ready gods. Degrees and letters and titles can become idols…Still another image men worship is that of power and prestige…*¹⁰

As we've discussed, art seems to have a power that—perhaps even more than other hobbies or avocations—captures our hearts and can overtake us. In this state, we can become centered on creation rather than Christ.

Traps

Another trap we fall into is that we often center our motives *for* creation and pursuing our artistic endeavors for worldly reasons, to the exclusion of Christ and His gospel. In the eternal picture, choosing another center matters a lot because it is a measure of what we love, and "…what we love determines what we seek. What we seek determines what we think and do. What we think and do determines who we are—and who we will become."[11] The center of our life and creation determines what it, in turn, will create in the world around us.

Christocentric Creation

What does it really mean to center our lives on Christ?

Martin Luther, the great sixteenth-century reformer, advocated what he called a Christocentric or Christ-centered theology. I would advocate what I call Christocentric Creation, or artistic work centered on Jesus Christ and His message to the world.

Does Christocentric mean we have to say His name in all of our songs and works of literature? Does it mean we have to include depictions of the Savior in all our paintings? No. Christ can speak through our creation without our having to say His name or paint His face.

All Things Which Are Good

How can all of our creation be Christocentric? Consider the following passage:

> *He comprehendeth all things, and all things are before him, and all things are round about him; and he is above all things, and in all things, and is through all things, and is round about all things; and all things are by him, and of him, even God, forever and ever.*[12]

When was the last time you took a moment to smell a flower, admire a sunset, listen to the music of birds or the swell of the ocean? Our creation can bear record of Him just as His creations bear record of Him[13] Christ can be in and through and round about all of our creation.

He can be the way, the truth and the life[14] of our creation. Paul taught, "Let this mind be in you, which was also in Christ Jesus."[15] As we develop more and more the "mind of Christ[16], as we pray that our performance will be consecrated[17], as we seek to "square all things in Christ,"[18] and as we seek to use all of our time, talents and energy for the building up of the Kingdom of God, our creation will bear record of Christ.

How can you tell?

In his remarkable talk "Centering the Arts in Christ," Former Brigham Young University professor of music, K. Newell Dayley listed some of the characteristics of art that is centered in Christ:

> *Art that is centered in Christ…*
>
> 1. *"Inviteth and enticeth to do good continually…to love God, and to serve him"* (Moroni 7:13).
> 2. *Persuades us 'to believe in Christ'* (Moroni 7:16).

3. *Seeks the welfare of Zion through service motivated by the pure love of Christ* (see 2 Nephi 26:29-31).
4. *Plants joy in the hearts of those who are seeking to be like Christ* (2 Nep. 2:25).
5. *Is virtuous and full of charity toward all men* (see D&C 121:45).
6. *Radiates light and is filled with hope* (see Moroni 7:48).
7. *Is born of meekness and lowliness of heart. The pure love of Christ is its driving force* (see Moroni 7:44-47; 8:25-26).
8. *Invites "the visitation of the Holy Ghost, which Comforter filleth with hope and perfect love"* (Moroni 8:26).
9. *Is created by those who, through faith in Christ, "shall have the power to do whatsoever thing is expedient in [Him]"* (Moroni 7:33).
10. *Is miraculous in its manifestation of beauty and love.*
11. *Is created by those who desire to "come unto Christ, and be perfected in him, and deny [themselves] of all ungodliness...and love God with all [their] might, mind and strength...that by his grace [they] may be perfect in Christ"* (Moroni 10:32).
12. *Is manifest according to the power of the Holy Ghost* (see 2 Nephi 32:2-5).[19]

But what about artists like me who are required to perform a (clean) tribute to Michael Jackson 200 times a year? What about artists who make a living as the lead singer of a rock band? What about talk show hosts and authors who don't speak about or write about gospel topics? It's not as easy to see these artistic endeavors being centered in Christ, yet they serve a very useful purpose in building up the Lord's Kingdom. Allow me to share three liberating **characteristics of Christocentric Creation** that I have discovered as I've wrestled with these questions.

#1 – For the Benefit of the World: The Leader-Servant Mentality

Dr. C. Raymond Smith is the director of Jazz Studies at BYU and he has toured internationally as director of Synthesis, the university's highly successful jazz ensemble. Listen to what he had to say about Christocentric Creation in jazz:

> *My model is the Savior. How would the Savior handle performing? That's been my goal for many years…Could I play with humility and yet confidence born of that humility and the same love and compassion…that the Savior would play if he were playing my part?*

What are your thoughts so far? Had you ever considered approaching a genre like jazz this way? Carefully consider how he continues:

> *So I'll start by reading scriptures and do some pondering, and then that'll lead me into prayer where I ask the Lord to help me grapple with these conflicting motives and to have my motives pure…When that really happens, the Spirit can actuate us in ways that we really could never do on our own. Performances can be more exhilarating, and more energetic, more focused than ever. So many years I did that before performances; it's almost become a way of life…It's about service.*[20]

I think Dr. Smith is on to something here. Christocentric Creation is about service. It's about pure motives. In the Book of Mormon Nephi teaches us about Christ's motives:

> *For behold, my beloved brethren, I say unto you that the Lord God worketh not in darkness. He doeth not anything save it be for the benefit of the world; for he loveth the world, even that he layeth down his own life that he may draw all men unto him.*[21]

If Christ is to be the lodestar in all of our artistic endeavors, then it would be wise to pattern our motives after His. What are his motives?

Arian's story

Arian, a TAD 101 graduate, shared a story that sheds some light on the kind of motives Christ has:

> *While struggling through a very difficult time, I dropped to my knees and pled with the Lord for strength. This was a Saturday night. The next day in church, our closing hymn was "Be Still, My Soul." The Spirit opened up my heart and poured the words in until I couldn't sing any more for all the tears streaming down my face. I understood each phrase as though I was hearing it for the first time, and it gave me an almost tangible sense of hope and strength. I knew my prayer was being answered.*
>
> *After church I felt like I should to talk with my bishop, so I waited until he was available for a brief chat. I told him how much the hymns had touched me that day, especially "Be Still, My Soul." He said, "This hymn wasn't on the program last night when it was about to be printed. While I was reviewing the program for today, it was clear to me that the closing hymn needed to be changed to "Be Still, My Soul." So I changed it, and now I know why. It was for you."*
>
> *I knew in that moment that the Lord had heard my prayer, answered me, and wanted me to know exactly how He had done it. His Spirit taught me powerfully through a sweet, beautiful hymn. I remember His deep love for me now every time I sing it.*

How often have you and I heard about and experienced similar things? As we know, the Savior does nothing save it be for the benefit of the world because He loves the world and He loves us. I will even suggest that the Lord gives us no *personal* revelation save it be for the ultimate benefit of the *world*, whether that is for one person or a whole congregation.

How can we adopt this leader-servant mentality in all of our creation?

One idea is to ask ourselves the following question when we are lit with the spark of creative inspiration: "How can this idea benefit the world?"

The leader-servant[22] mentality is exocentric—it seeks to benefit the world, not ourselves. Thomas Edison had a similar philosophy:

> *I never perfected an invention that I did not think about in terms of the service it might give others. I find out what the world needs, then I proceed to invent.*[23]

From a purely economic standpoint, Edison's philosophy makes sense. Why create something the world doesn't need? There won't be any market for it. From a spiritual standpoint it makes even more sense. Benefitting and serving the temporal needs of the world is a noble purpose. Benefitting and serving the spiritual needs of the world is even nobler.

Welfare of Souls

George Frederic Handel once had a man approach him after the performance of his music and congratulate him on an "entertaining" concert. What do you think Handel had in mind when he replied, "My lord, I should be sorry that I only entertained them. I wish to make them better"?[24]

Heber J. Grant once instructed Spencer W. Kimball, "Set your heart upon the service of the Lord thy God. From this very moment, resolve to make this cause and this labor first and foremost in all your thoughts." As we seek to serve God and His children, to build up the Kingdom first and foremost in all our thoughts and creative work, and as our motives are based in love, our creation will be Christocentric. We will, like Lehi, "have none other object save it be the everlasting welfare of...souls,"[25] and our creation will reflect this Leader-Servant Mentality.

#2 – Christocentric Creation is Transformational Creation

What is Transformational Creation?

As Artist-Disciples, we are in the business of transforming people. David O. McKay said, "The gospel exists to make bad men good, and good men better, and to change human nature."[26]

Transformational Creation has the same objective. It always seeks, at least in some way, to lead men and women along the eternal progression continuum from telestial to terrestrial to celestial—whether it be an inch or a mile. Sometimes it speaks directly of Christ, but often it is for the purpose of drawing others to *us* so they can learn.

What about Michael?

Remember the questions posed earlier about those of us who make a living in supposedly "secular" areas? So much of it is about purpose and motives. I have many reasons for performing a tribute to Michael Jackson in our family variety show. Here are some of them:

- To entertain our audience (that's what I'm paid for).
- To show the audience that you can still be entertaining without performing the inappropriate moves (I get positive comments about that all the time).

- To get the audience in the door in the first place! Although we haven't tried it, they probably won't come to a show called *The Bretts' Gospel-Sharing Time Show.*
- To keep the audience captivated and engaged enough so that they will be ready to hear our message when that time comes in the show. People listen to and believe people they know, like, and trust. Part of the strategy of performing a Michael Jackson tribute is to help the audience know, like, trust and respect our craftsmanship enough to listen to what comes from our heart later on.

Not all creative work need be of a celestial nature to have transformational power. In some way, my Michael Jackson performance prepares people to be moved along the eternal progression spectrum—to be transformed. That is its strategic purpose within our show. Plus, I have to admit, it's a lot of fun to do and I'm always thrilled when the audience roars at the end of my performance.

An Example

I had the opportunity once to visit with a man who has had a huge impact on the values, morals and practices of the world. He was a Latter-day Saint, but he was best known in the world for his contribution outside the Church. During our conversation, he shared with me his life mission. He felt that his work was to be a terrestrial work—to teach people the gospel without them knowing they were being taught the gospel. He felt that he could be, like John the Baptist, a forerunner to prepare the way for the Second Coming. Many Latter-Day Saints find their life work in this category, and many more are being prepared to do so.

There Are Millions...

Do some of us tend to think that if our work isn't celestial work (i.e. teaching the gospel directly, temple work, baptizing, teaching seminary or institute, etc.) that it isn't as valuable? It is true that participating directly in the work of salvation is the most important thing, but we need to remember that there are many ways to do it. Doctrinally speaking, terrestrial work is not wasted effort at all. Elder Charles A. Callis had this to say about the Second Coming:

> *Now brethren and sisters, the great day of the Lord is coming...The wicked are going to be destroyed, and when I say the wicked I do not mean everybody outside the Mormon Church. There will be countless millions of people not of this Church spared because they are not ripe in iniquity and to them we will preach the everlasting Gospel and bring them unto Christ.*[27]

As Artist-Disciples seeking to produce Transformational Creation and form a new Upstream, we can be instrumental in teaching some of those "countless millions" the eternal and universal truths of the gospel, which will help them progress toward—not necessarily to—celestial glory. We can teach them the gospel without them knowing they're being taught the gospel. And again, we don't have to preach to people to have Christ in our creation.

What is your goal?

The following is an excerpt of a review our show received on TripAdvisor.com; intended to be illustrative, not self-promotional:

> *I am never disappointed by the performance of [The Bretts]... Unlike some of the shows that "preach" at you, you can see the Bretts' faith on display by simply listening to them.*[28]

For me, this was one of the highest compliments we could have received because it was exactly what we were after—Transformational Creation. Transformational Creation is purpose-driven. It asks the questions "Why do you create?" as well as "What is the goal of your art?"

Mick Jagger had a goal. He achieved fame, but I would hate to have the consequences of that kind of fame. Like him, if our purpose is selfish, then our true creativity will be limited and our ability to positively influence people through our creation will be severely impaired.

A purpose or center such as fame or making money will influence the things we create, the jobs we will take, and ultimately the impact and level of self-satisfaction we have. If we really want to transform lives and make a difference through our creation, then we must have a transformational Christocentric creative focus.

Transformational Creation is immersed in higher purpose. It is as deep as theology, as provocative as philosophy, as precise as science. It is supremely spiritually-rooted. As we will discuss more in Chapter 8, Transformational Creation is vital to our success, both as an artist and as a disciple.

#3 – Christocentric Creation: "As to the Lord"

A third liberating characteristic of Christocentric Creation I'd like to share comes from two great Christians: the Apostle Paul and C.S. Lewis.

Here is Paul's take on it, from his instruction to servants as recorded in Ephesians: "Servants, be obedient to them that are your masters according to the flesh...*as unto Christ;* Not...as men pleasers; but as the servants of Christ, doing the will of God from the heart...*as to the*

Lord, and not to men:"²⁹ What is the significance of this teaching as it relates to Christocentric Creation?

C.S. Lewis has some thoughts. Consider this excerpt from his essay, *Learning in War-Time*:

> *I believe that our whole life can, and indeed must, become religious in a sense…Before I became a Christian I do not think I fully realized that one's life, after conversion, would inevitably consist in doing most of the same things one had been doing before: one hopes, in a new spirit, but still the same things…Neither conversion nor enlistment in the army is really going to obliterate our human life. Christians and soldiers are still men…Christianity does not exclude any of the ordinary human activities…*

Here we could replace "Christianity" with, "becoming an Artist-Disciple," "joining a band," "painting a masterpiece," etc. Now watch his use of the phrase in question as he continues:

> *The solution of this paradox is, of course, well known to you. "Whether ye eat or drink or whatsoever ye do, do all to the glory of God." All our merely natural activities will be accepted, if they are offered to God, even the humblest: and all of them, even the noblest, will be sinful if they are not. Christianity does not simply replace our natural life and substitute a new one: it is rather a new organization which exploits, to its own supernatural ends, these natural materials.…<u>The work of a Beethoven, and the work of a charwoman, become spiritual on precisely the same condition, that of being offered to God, of being done humbly "as to the Lord."</u>³⁰*

For me this teaching is profound. Just because we are members of the Church does not mean we are excluded from the normal activities of human life. It is not expected of all of us to forsake our lead-singer job in a rock band and become seminary teachers—although there is nothing wrong with doing that. The point here is that our work, no matter what it is, becomes holy on the principle of "being done humbly 'as to the Lord.'"

Joy in Every Second

The principle of serving the Lord in all we do is magnified in the following story told by BYU Professor, Brother Jeffery Thompson. He describes nearing the end of his mission and feeling sorrow for the fact that he would no longer be a full-time servant of the Lord. His zone had a Q&A with their mission president.

> *I raised my hand and asked, "After our missions are over and we are no longer full-time servants of God, how can we keep a sense of purpose?" Before the mission president could answer, his wife leapt to her feet and, literally elbowing him aside, said, "I'll take this one."*
>
> *I will never forget her response. As near as I can recall, she said, "When I do the laundry, I am building the kingdom of God. When I scrub the floors, I am serving the Lord. When I tidy the clutter, I'm an instrument in His hands. I do a lot of mundane jobs, but if my eye is single to God and I'm trying to serve my family, then I feel as much purpose in my work as a missionary can.*[31]

These words resonate with me as well. If we truly lived our lives with this mind and heart-set, we would find joy and purpose in every second. Of course, just because we are converted to Christianity, and are performing our work "as to the Lord," does not exempt us from the necessities, realities and vicissitudes of mortality. As Lewis said in another article, "The cross comes before the crown and tomorrow is a Monday morning."[32] There will be many Monday mornings and challenges in our lives and in our creative processes.

However, if we adopt this "as to the Lord" mentality, in combination with the other two liberating characteristics mentioned above, all of our creation can be Christocentric. If we understand the integrated and holistic nature of the gospel of Jesus Christ, we will realize that there is really no separation between our work and His work if our hearts are right before Him. We would do well to capitalize the "w" in work and turn every second of every day into Work—His work and His glory.

Finding the Lodestar

What will it take to make Christ the "Lodestar of your life"?

For me, it is a daily, concerted effort to allow Him to be in and through and round about all of my Three Rings, including my artistic endeavors. As I have done this, I have found profound examples of His help in my creation. Without His help, it would be so easy to get lost in the secular smog and be carried about by every wind of trend or doctrine; not making a positive and Kingdom-building impact.

I testify that Christ is the source of my energy, my light, my vision, and my creativity. I testify that He strengthens, inspires, encourages, and gives us grace as we seek to make Him and His gospel the Lodestar of our lives and our creation. I know that putting Him first will ensure that everything works out in the most eternally beneficial way for us and those we influence.

After all, if we are going to navigate the stormy waters of the Mainstream towards a new and beautiful Upstream, who better to show us the way to than the Lodestar?

> **Questions and Action Items:**
>
> 1. How does keeping an eye single to the glory of God qualify you for the work of creation?
>
> 2. How can the worship of your artistic work become idolatry?
>
> 3. How can your artistic work become as praise to God, even if He is not mentioned directly?

Chapter Summary

- Christ must be the lodestar of our lives and of our creative work.
- There are many centers in life that compete for our loyalty, but Christ must always remain our primary center. We must live Christocentrically and create Christocentrically.
- When we produce Christocentric Creation, Christ can be in and through everything we create. Christocentric Creation is the best creation and has the following three liberating characteristics:
    - #1 – It seeks to benefit the world. Christocentric Creation is created by Artist-Disciples who have a leader-servant mentality.
    - #2 – Christocentric Creation is Transformational Creation. It seeks to produce positive progress in people by helping them move along the eternal progression continuum from telestial to terrestrial to celestial.
    - #3 – As Artist-Disciples we are not exempt from the daily and mundane activities of normal existence and not all of our creative work will seem celestial. But, as long as we dedicate our lives and our creative work "as

to the Lord," all of our work can be part of His work.

---

[1] Personal interview with the author.
[2] Merriam-Webster Online Dictionary, merriam-webster.com/dictionary/lodestar.
[3] Helaman 5:12.
[4] 3 Nephi 13:33.
[5] Brigham Young, as quoted by The Church of Jesus Christ of Latter-day Saints, *Teachings of Presidents of the Church: Brigham Young*, 12.
[6] Lawrence M. Barry, "Marriage and the Law of the Harvest," *Liahona*, Aug.-Sep. 1986.
[7] Ezra Taft Benson, "The Great Commandment –Love the Lord," *Ensign*, May 1988.
[8] Exodus 20:3-4.
[9] Merriam-Webster Online Dictionary, merriam-webster.com/dictionary/idolatry.
[10] Spencer W. Kimball, *Teachings of Spencer W. Kimball*, 146-7.
[11] Dieter F. Uchtdorf, "The Love of God," *Ensign*, November 2009.
[12] Doctrine and Covenants 88:41.
[13] Alma 30:44; Moses 6:63.
[14] John 14:6.
[15] Philippians 2:5.
[16] 1 Corinthians 2:16.
[17] 2 Nephi 32:2-3.
[18] Ephesians 1:10.
[19] K. Newell Dayley, "Centering the Arts in Christ," BYU Devotional, March 6, 2001.
[20] Nicole Sheahan, "Inside Mormon Music: a look back at 'Inside Mormon Music'," deseretnews.com/article/705387050/A-look-back-at-Inside-Mormon-Music.html?pg=all.
[21] 2 Nephi 26:23-24.
[22] Neal A. Maxwell, "Spencer, the Beloved: Leader-Servant," *Ensign*, December 1985.
[23] Thomas Edison, thomasedison.com/quotes.html.
[24] George Frederic Handel, as quoted by Marinella F. Monk, *Gentle Therapy*, 184.
[25] 2 Nephi 2:30.
[26] David O. McKay, goodreads.com/author/quotes/601416.David_O_McKay.
[27] Charles A. Callis, as quoted by The Church of Jesus Christ of Latter-day Saints, *Doctrines of the Gospel Student Manual*, 102.
[28] S. David, Visited The Bretts Show in June 2012, tripadvisor.com/ShowUserReviews-g44160-d2332145-r132852114-The_Bretts-Branson_Missouri.html#REVIEWS.

[29] Ephesians 6:5-7, emphasis added.
[30] C.S. Lewis, "Learning in War-Time," 7, emphasis added.
[31] Jeffery A. Thompson, "What is Your Calling in Life?" *BYU Magazine*, Spring 2011.
[32] C.S. Lewis, goodreads.com/quotes/160392-the-cross-comes-before-the-crown-and-tomorrow-is-a.

Lesson 6:
The X Factor

Artist-Disciple Insights

Michelle's Story: After the Trial of Your Faith

I tried really hard to get into The School of Fine Arts at Kansas University. There were applications, essays, referrals, portfolio, interviews, transferring and petitioning all my credits from other schools. It was a lot of work and a lot of time spent, but all my hard work paid off because I was one of 5 that got accepted that year.

I loved school! I did really well at it. I loved the quick growth. However, for some reason I felt like I shouldn't be there. I was upset with this feeling because it contradicted what I wanted. I prayed about it several times and got no answer or direction on what to do. I talked to my family and friends about it, fasted and prayed more and still, no answer.

Time came to enroll in the next semester. It was very scary to think about quitting or failing or losing what I worked so hard for. I kept praying for understanding and guidance to know what to do and still no answer… but still had the feeling like I shouldn't go to school. It was the very last day to pay for classes, and with very little confidence I pulled out of my classes. I felt very sad and alone and didn't understand why Heavenly Father was not answering me.

As I sat there sad and crying, I felt this overwhelming feeling of love and comfort. I felt my Father in Heaven so close to me. I really felt him wrap his arms around me. I felt his unconditional love. I knew that I had listened to him and had done what was right. He without a doubt then answered my prayers. I knew after this that his plan for me was better than the plan I had for myself. I for sure had worries of not progressing BUT I trusted him and I am glad I did.

I'm glad I obeyed because (6 years later) I am still receiving blessings from that choice. Shortly after I trusted that small feeling and pulled out of school, many opportunities were presented to me. Here are just a few...

- *I was asked to be the head graphic designer at a design firm (even though most people have to finish school to get this position).*
- *I was approached to be a storyboard artist for a movie production company.*
- *Someone requested that I do a commissioned charcoal drawing. Today this drawing is my best-selling piece.*
- *I was then invited to work for a law firm for several years doing all their business cards, logos, advertisements, billboards etc.*
- *I never applied for a job, yet I had options and opportunities of where I could work.*
- *I did not have a degree but yet employers were raising my pay so that I would leave where I was to come work for them.*

God showed me how much he loves me and how much he cares about not only me, but what I want. When I think of this experience I think of the scripture Ether 12:6, which talks about how faith is things hoped for and not seen, for ye receive no witness until AFTER the trial of your faith. God waited for me to make the choice. It was AFTER the trial, after I pulled out of school, that I was blessed.

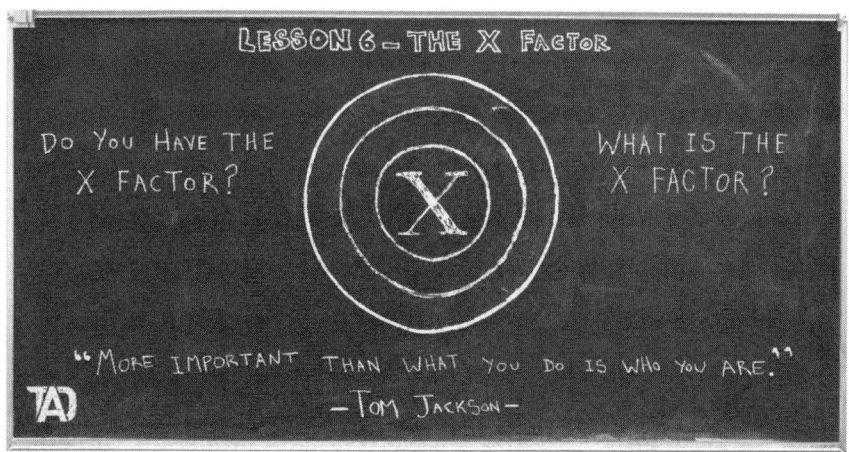

And the winner is...

Not too long ago I had the opportunity to attend a live taping of auditions for Simon Cowell's latest reality TV enterprise here in the USA, *The X Factor*. *The X Factor* is like *American Idol* on steroids—a bigger and edgier spinoff of the original hit TV series with a different set of rules, a different panel of judges, and everything done on a much larger scale.

The audition I attended featured about twenty individual acts auditioning in front of 8,000 people at the Sprint Center in Kansas City, MO. Britney Spears, Demi Lovato, Antonio L.A. Reid, and Simon Cowell were the judging panel looking for the next big star who had "the X factor"—that elusive blend of secret sauce that catapults artists into stardom. The whole experience led me to ponder about this whole idea of having the X factor.

Forming the Upstream, X Factor-style

What is the X factor? I think I like this definition best:

> *X Factor – That unknown factor, or the unexplainable thing, which adds a certain value to an object, element or person; in*

relation to a person it is defined as the unexplainable element of a person's attractiveness.[1]

Today's lesson is about the X factor for Artist-Disciples—that hopefully (fingers crossed) explainable element of an Artist-Disciple's attractiveness which adds value to him or her and to all he or she creates. This is my take on what it will take to change the world through our artistic endeavors. Developing the X factor is an important step in forming the Upstream.

Character vs. Personality

In order to understand the X factor for Artist-Disciples, it will be important to cover two terms from Dr. Stephen R. Covey's landmark book, *The 7 Habits of Highly Effective People*—Character Ethic and Personality Ethic.

Character Ethic (CE) = Disciple

Dr. Covey uncovered the concept of the Character Ethic during his study of the success literature published in the United States since 1776, or about 200 years worth of material. During the first 150 years of literature, he noticed that the common view of success focused on what he called the Character Ethic:

> *...things like integrity, humility, fidelity, temperance, courage, justice, patience, industry, simplicity, modesty, and the Golden Rule... The Character Ethic taught that there are basic principles of effective living, and that people can only experience true success and enduring happiness as they learn and integrate these principles into their basic character.*[2]

The Character Ethic is more intangible and focuses on your character, your motives, your attributes and your nature—who you are.

Personality Ethic (PE) = Artist

Let's continue with Dr. Covey's narrative:

> ...*Shortly after World War I, the basic view of success shifted from the Character Ethic to what we might call the Personality Ethic. Success became more a function of personality, of public image, of attitudes and behaviors, skills and techniques that lubricate the processes of human interaction...Reference to the Character Ethic became mostly lip service; the basic thrust was quick-fix influence techniques, power strategies, communication skills, and positive attitudes.*[3]

The Personality Ethic is more tangible and focuses on your techniques, your skills, your strategies and your craft—what you do.

For our purposes today I am going to refer to the Character Ethic as **who you are**. It is the *disciple* side of Artist-Disciple. I will refer to the Personality Ethic a little more positively than Dr. Covey did and classify it as **what you do**. It is the *artist* side of Artist-Disciple. Neither is bad and neither is necessarily better than the other. Actually, in order to be a true Artist-Disciple you must have both CE and PE. But which one is the X factor?

Character Ethic

Since the world tends to neglect the Character Ethic, that is where we will begin and where we will spend the largest amount of time in this lesson. In Lesson 4, we discussed Ring #1: our purpose is to *become* like Heavenly Father and Jesus Christ. We also introduced the topic of *becoming*. Now it is time to go a little deeper because *becoming* is what the Character Ethic is all about. As with other topics in this course, *becoming* is a book itself, so we will cover it broadly as it relates to Artist-Discipleship.

Being, Doing, Knowing

Becoming involves the process of knowing, doing and ultimately being; it is a habitual way of thinking, acting and feeling. It is the process of conversion, of being transformed. President Henry B. Eyring teaches that our objective is to "…find the way in this life to have our natures changed through the Atonement of Jesus Christ."[4]

Becoming is creation. It is who we are deep down inside. Everything in the gospel exists to help us *become* like Jesus Christ—to be a heavenly *being* like He is. I believe that no one has taught the principle of becoming more clearly than Elder Dallin H. Oaks:

> *…It is not even enough for us to be <u>convinced</u> of the gospel; we must act and think so that we are <u>converted</u> by it. In contrast to the institutions of the world, which teach us to <u>know</u> something, the gospel of Jesus Christ challenges us to <u>become</u> something…We conclude that the Final Judgment is not just an evaluation of a sum total of good and evil acts—what we have <u>done</u>. It is an acknowledgment of the final effect of our acts and thoughts— what we have <u>become</u>. It is not enough for anyone just to go through the motions. The commandments, ordinances, and covenants of the gospel are not a list of deposits required to be made in some heavenly account. The gospel of Jesus Christ is a plan that shows us how to <u>become</u> what our Heavenly Father desires us to <u>become</u>.*[5]

Like the Character Ethic, *becoming* involves our motives, our hearts, our character, our nature and our very core self. We are to put off the natural man and become a saint through the Atonement of Christ the Lord.[6]

The pickle says it all

I love Elder David A. Bednar's "Parable of the Pickle" as it relates to becoming. A cucumber becomes a pickle through prolonged immersion in brine. As we fully saturate ourselves in the gospel, the journey of mortality changes us from bad to good, from good to better, from telestial cucumbers to celestial pickles. "Through faith in Christ we can be spiritually prepared and cleansed from sin, immersed and saturated with His gospel, and purified and sealed by the Holy Spirit of Promise."[7]

Becoming is a process of spiritual rebirth made possible through the Atonement of Jesus Christ. It is both the redeeming power and the divine enabling power (grace) of Christ that make it possible for us to have our natures changed. He has paid the debt and opened the door in every way for us to follow in His footsteps and become like Him. In all of this, what we *do* is important but, as President Eyring observed, "The things we do are the means, not the end we seek. What we do allows the Atonement of Jesus Christ to change us into what we must be."[8]

Who are you, really?

So, why does all of this becoming and Character Ethic stuff matter to Artist-Disciples? Consider this story:

At *The X Factor* auditions I mentioned earlier, there was one audition that really caught my attention. It was an audition by a middle-aged woman from the Midwest who had been singing her entire life. Beaten down and told she could never make it as a singer, she had almost given up on her dream. But here she was on *The X Factor* stage in front of thousands (and eventually millions on TV) of people.

As was common with all participants, the judges asked her a series of questions before her performance. When she spoke I could feel a depth and breadth in her soul that came from years of hard work, pain and experience. I literally felt the Spirit as she spoke. Her Character Ethic connected with me and with thousands of people in that audience. You could tell she meant what she said. More importantly, you could tell she *was* what she said. She had me. She had all of us, and we were pulling for her. We wanted her to win.

Such is the power of becoming. Your audience may not be experts in the technical elements of music, acting, painting, literature or whatever creative field you're involved in, but they are experts in the sub-conscious sense of feeling—of feeling who you are. When your system of motives and your character is pure and full of passion, it sends a palpable energy from you to your audience and infuses your creation with a breadth and depth that can be felt.

What sets us apart?

I have experienced this phenomenon myself as a performer. I hear comments every time I do a show with my family. People talk about the different "feeling" they had at our show. They talk about how our performance came from our heart. They can really *feel* a difference that they can't often explain. But we know where this difference comes from: it is the power of the Spirit; it is the power of the Atonement; and it is also the power and purity they feel coming from our being—from who we are.

Music producer Tom Jackson put it this way, "On stage, more important than what you do is who you are."[9] Elder Lynn G. Robbins said, "Christlike to be's cannot be seen, but they are the motivating force behind what we do, which can be seen."[10] And, I would add, they are a motivating force that can be felt (even if only on a subconscious level) by everyone who is exposed to you and your art.

President David O. McKay amplified this teaching when he instructed gospel teachers that, "The great influencing factor in the classroom is the teacher; his personality, what he thinks, not just what he says, but *what he is, really and truly in his heart*—this is what influences his students."[11] The same is true of us as Artist-Disciples. As we strive to develop Christlike attributes and as our motives and natures become transformed into Christ's motives and nature, people will feel the difference in our art. They will feel a difference in our performance.

Time to Be Converted

Another reason why Character Ethic matters so much to Artist-Disciples is encapsulated in this statement by President James E. Faust: "You cannot convert people beyond your own conversion."[12] We can't lift others to higher ground unless we are on higher ground ourselves. We lead others to Christ to the extent we are being led by Him. If we refuse to put Him first or modify our plans to fit His plan, who are we to guide those around us to Him?

As we deepen and widen who we are, more people will be attracted to us[13] and we will be enabled to direct them to higher ground. As we serve others, we will often experience the additional blessing of finding that those we help aren't the only ones being helped. This old proverb seems to hold true, "Thee lift me and I'll lift thee and we shall ascend together."[14] We will be lifted as we seek to lift.

Prepared For the Eternities

Finally, the most important reason why the Character Ethic should matter to Artist-Disciples is that, spiritually speaking, the Character Ethic—who you are—is the X factor. It is the sum total of the gospel. Elder Joseph B. Wirthlin taught, "The gospel of Jesus Christ is a gospel of transformation. It takes us as men and women of the earth and refines us into men and women for the eternities."[15] If we miss the boat of becoming "men and women for the eternities," then we miss the purpose of life. Artistically speaking, the Character Ethic is also part of the X factor. It can be the intangible thing that will give that unexplainable magic to what we do as artists.

Elder Maxwell taught, "All of us are in the process of becoming—including prophets and General Authorities."[16] I'm grateful for that reassurance because, as I write this, I realize that I have a long way to go. We have a great challenge to live up to our theology.

Yet, the rewards for striving to live up to what we believe are obvious. Focusing on the Character Ethic by seeking the mighty change of heart we've discussed today will not only prepare us for eternity, but it will transform us to create art of transcendent value and improve all of our abilities as Artist-Disciples as we have discussed. Do you believe this? How can you become more focused on becoming like Jesus Christ? What steps do you need to take to improve your Character Ethic?

Personality Ethic

One of my favorite commercials as a child was Tim Hardaway and Spike Lee advertising Nike. Tim Hardaway would drain a three-pointer or shake a defender with his "killer crossover" and then turn to the camera and say, "I got skills."

Do you "got skills?"

As important as the Character Ethic is, as an Artist-Disciple, it's also vital that we have skills.

To illustrate this point, let's continue our story of the inspiring Midwestern soul singer from *The X Factor* auditions. As I mentioned earlier, her Character Ethic had all of us pulling for her and eating out of the palm of her hand. Everyone was on the edge of their seat waiting to see if her skills could deliver on the great expectation we were all feeling coming from her heart. Her music track started, she stepped up to the microphone to sing, and (drum roll please)…it wasn't all that great. I don't want to sound too harsh, but her skills were not on the same level as her heart, and I could tell the crowd was disappointed. We all shifted our attention to the next contestant, hoping to find the artist with the X factor.

This experience illustrates the fickleness of audiences for sure, but it also illustrates something else. It shows us the need that audiences have to feel Character Ethic and see Personality Ethic. Because her Personality Ethic had not caught up with her Character Ethic quite yet, the audience was left wanting.

Now, the good news is that she made it through to the next round and I remember hoping that she would go far as she worked with the producers to develop her skills. But this was a very illuminating experience that helped me understand the importance of the Personality Ethic for an Artist-Disciple.

Superior or Stinks?

I think this humorous statement by Steve Lawrence of the comedy duo "Steve and Eydie" applies to the principle of Personality Ethic pretty well: "…you can't be in the music business as long as 'Steve and Eydie' have, if you stink…"[17]

President Spencer W. Kimball spoke to BYU faculty and encouraged them to achieve in both the secular and spiritual realms. He promised them that they would be more respected by their students if they did. "You can, in fact, often be more effective in the service you render students if students see you as individuals who have blended successfully things secular and things spiritual in a way that has brought to you earned respect in both realms."[18]

People respect you more if you have achieved in both the Character Ethic and the Personality Ethic, in both the spiritual and secular realms. In the world of artistic creation, people expect you not to stink.

Now I realize that what people think "stinks" varies and is subject to subjective aesthetic opinions, but there is no denying that people respond to excellence and achievement. Because we will spend an entire chapter on this topic later, I will not expound too much on this principle now. These infrastructural principles will frame our discussion later and help us move toward a final conclusion on what the X factor really is.

What is the X Factor?

I believe that to be all that you can be as an Artist-Disciple requires a balance of the Personality Ethic and the Character Ethic. To illustrate this principle, let's revise our Upstream diagram from Lesson 3 a little bit:

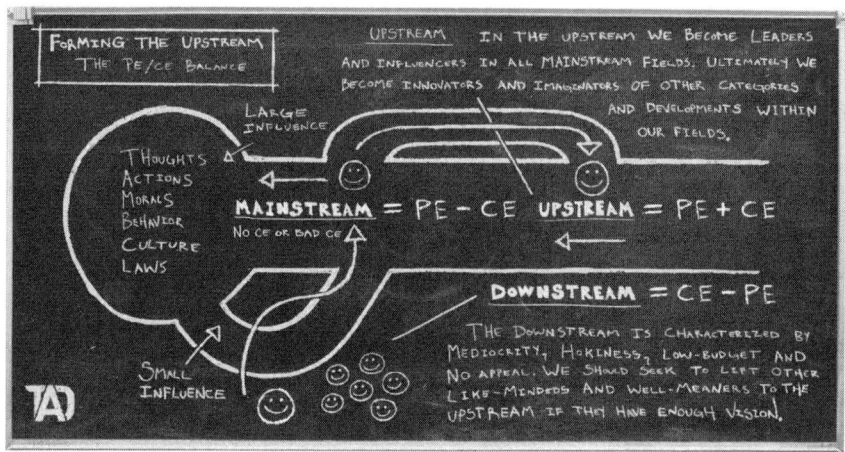

In the Downstream you see a lot of artists and people who possess a lot of the Character Ethic characteristics but who don't have very many of the Personality Ethic characteristics—good hearts but not a lot of skills. They are not masters of their craft and they don't seem to get as big a response from their audiences.

In the Mainstream you see a lot of artists with a lot of Personality Ethic but very little Character Ethic. This combination seems to be more popular since the artists can at least put on the superficial trappings of Personality Ethic (i.e. techniques, skills, strategies, resources, etc.) to which people respond. These artists tend to be more masterful at their craft. They "got skills," and, consequently, they have audiences.

Even more dangerously, as in the case of Mick Jagger, some Mainstream artists have Personality Ethic and the wrong or ill-motivated Character Ethic. There is real power in *becoming*, even if what you become is not righteous. People respond to passion and purpose when they feel it in an artist's life and work.

Lastly, in the Upstream is where you will find the PE/CE Balance—the balanced combination of Personality Ethic and the right, or pure-motivated, Character Ethic. These are the types of artists who produce transformational creation. People respond to your heart *and* to your skills. For Artist-Disciples, this is the X factor. It is not one or the other. It is the combination of the two:

PE + CE = The X Factor

Artistry & Discipleship – A Pull All Together

So how do you develop the X factor?

Again, we will continue this discussion in later lessons, but here is one guiding principle from President Dieter F. Uchtdorf:

> *As a people, we rightfully place high priority on secular learning and vocational development. We want and we must excel in scholarship and craftsmanship. I commend you for striving diligently to gain an education and become an expert in your field. I invite you to also become experts in the doctrines of the gospel…*[19]

To me, what President Uchtdorf is saying as it relates to the topic at hand is that discipleship should always run ahead of craftsmanship. The spiritual should always run ahead of the secular. President Uchtdorf himself is a living example of this. The disciple should always lead the artist. BUT, they must run together.

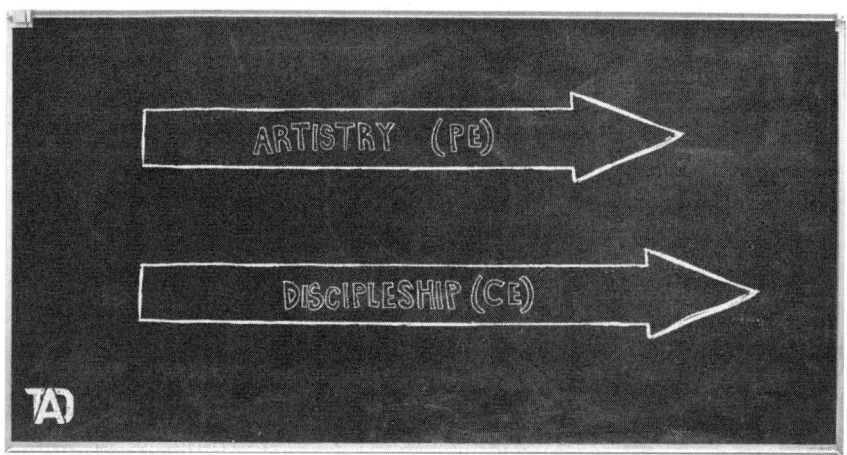

The secret in the term PE/CE Balance is the world "balance." It is not one or the other. We must never shut off the spiritual in favor of the secular. We see too many students and artists do this. It's almost like they rationalize in their minds, "Oh, I'll focus on the spiritual after I graduate college," or at the opposite extreme "I'll be an artist after my kids are grown and gone…I don't need to develop this talent now, it doesn't matter that much," or whatever the excuse may be.

While there are times and seasons in life for special focus on both, the key is to daily pull the two together, with discipleship always leading the way. If we let craftsmanship lead the way then we run into the problem we've discussed before—the Second Identity and Ring #3 take over and consume the other important identities and rings in our life.

If, on the other hand, we allow discipleship to frame and inform artistry, then we will develop as an Artist-Disciple much more efficiently. Discipleship and artistry, always improving in tandem, lead to power as an Artist-Disciple.

Step Up Your Daily

One of my favorite sayings is, "Details done daily determine the difference."

Daily is the key. In order for us to become the powerful Artist-Disciples we want to be, we get to invest daily time in both areas.

It is absolutely necessary as disciples of Jesus Christ that we seek daily to deepen our conversion and our becoming. It is also absolutely necessary as artists that we seek daily to master our craft, whatever our craft is. These two daily focuses will work synergistically to help us become powerful and effective Artist-Disciples faster.

Whatever your area of creation, I challenge you to step up your daily habits and practices of both disciple and artist. As you do so, divine help will surely follow.

Magnification by Grace

Does all this make you feel excited?

I realize that we've talked about some pretty high ideals so far. I hope it is inspiring to you, as it is to me. I also realize that there may be times when understanding how we can have an impact in both artistry and discipleship may be just a bit overwhelming. Can you relate?

We know that perfection is a step-by-step process. Although there will be smaller goals to achieve along the way, we don't do ourselves any favors when we strive for anything less than the ideal. At the very least, we must start from the bottom of the ladder with the top in our view.

With this in mind, I'd like to share a concluding thought about a principle I call magnification by grace.

What did you sow today?

Lawrence Berry said that "at any given moment, we are the sum of all our sowings."[20] There is a lot of scientific justice in this statement. The eminent American psychologist William James said something similar,

> The Hell to be endured hereafter, of which theology tells, is no worse than the hell we make for ourselves in this world by habitually fashioning our characters in the wrong way… We are spinning our own fate, good or evil and never to be undone. Every smallest stroke of virtue or of vice leaves its never so little scar.
>
> The drunken Rip Van Winkle in Jefferson's play excuses himself every fresh dereliction by saying "I won't count this time." Well, he may not count it and a kind Heaven may not count it, but it is being counted nonetheless. Down among his nerve cells and fibers the molecules are counting it, registering it and storing it up to be used against him when the next temptation comes. Nothing we ever do is in a strict scientific literalness wiped out.
>
> Of course, this has its good side as well as its bad one. As we become permanent drunkards by so many separate drinks, so we become saints in the moral, and authorities and experts in the practical and scientific spheres by so many separate acts and hours of work.[21]

Wow. To me, this says that Artist-Discipleship is not achieved by one quick stroke of genius, but by the tiny, everyday things we do. Every thought, every word, every hour at the piano or in front of canvas helps makes us who we will ultimately become. Which direction are you going?

Amazing Grace

Do you, like I do, believe in both justice and the law of the harvest, *and* in mercy and the Lord's law of the harvest? Herein is the magnification by grace rule. Christ's mercy and grace maximize the results of our righteous decisions and minimize the consequences of our unrighteous decisions. Since Christ's Atonement is infinite, I believe this has application, not just to the final judgment, but to each and every day of our lives. Christ is always there pushing us, strengthening us and being our active Advocate with the Father. His grace constantly magnifies our weak efforts.

The Lord has always used the pattern described by Paul, "…God hath chosen the foolish things of the world to confound the wise; and God hath chosen the weak things of the world to confound the things which are mighty."[22] We can gain comfort and strength from this, knowing that "the foolishness of God is wiser than men; and the weakness of God is stronger than men."[23]

Christ's grace is sufficient for us. We might not have the perfect balance of *CE* and *PE,* but Christ does, and His grace is sufficient to strengthen us and magnify our imperfect efforts. We don't have to be perfect to produce great things—there are thousands of examples of that in ancient and modern art. President Packer once said,

> *…The greatest hymns and anthems have not been composed, nor have the greatest illustrations been set down, nor the poems written, nor the paintings finished. When they are produced, who will produce them? Will it be the most talented and the most highly trained among us? I rather think it will not. They will be produced by those who are the most inspired among us. Inspiration can come to those whose talents are barely adequate, and their contribution will be felt for generations; and the Church and kingdom of God will move forward just a little more easily because they have been here.*

> *Some of our most gifted people struggle to produce a work of art, hoping that it will be described by the world as masterpiece! Monumental! Epic! When in truth the simple, compelling theme of "I Am a Child of God" has moved and will move more souls to salvation than would such a work were they to succeed.*[24]

As Artist-Disciples, we are going to need His grace in order to produce creation that will make a lasting difference in the world. The small and simple things we do in weakness—in both our skills and our character—will then produce a far greater effect on the world than we ever could have imagined on our own.

Did you pass the audition?

Simply put, our X Factor is seeking as much as we can to put ourselves on the Lord's side in both being and doing, and achieving excellence both in our lives and in our craft. For Artist-Disciples, that is the "…unknown factor, or…unexplainable thing, which adds a certain value to an object, element or person;" Combined with the Lord's grace, this formula is poised to catapult us into the next level of Upstream. Are you ready?

Questions and Action Items:

1. What are the top three ways in which you could improve your artistic skills? How can you begin to implement them today?

2. What one area of your character, if strengthened, would immensely improve your offering? What are you doing, or what could you do, to begin strengthening your character in this area?

3. If you could only choose to implement one daily habit to advance your Artist-Discipleship, what would it be? How would that habit create transformational change in your discipleship and in your artistry?

Chapter Summary

- Character Ethic is the disciple side of Artist-Disciple and involves who you are deep down inside.
- Personality Ethic is the artist side of Artist-Disciple and involves what you do—your skills and craft as an artist.
- PE + CE = The X Factor; In other words, the balance of Character Ethic and Personality Ethic together is what gives you that extra magic as an artist and makes your creations stick in people's minds and hearts.
- Discipleship and artistry should be improving together daily with discipleship always leading the way.
- The magnification by grace rule tells us that Christ will maximize the results of our righteous decisions and minimize the consequences of our unrighteous decisions. This allows us, without the perfect PE/CE balance, to still produce art of transformational value.

[1] wiki.answers.com/Q/What_is_the_meaning_of_X_Factor.
[2] Steven R. Covey, *The 7 Habits of Highly Effective People*, 18.
[3] Covey, *The 7 Habits of Highly Effective People*, 19.
[4] Henry B. Eyring, "As a Child," *Ensign*, May 2006.
[5] Dallin H. Oaks, "The Challenge to Become," *Ensign*, November 2000.
[6] Mosiah 3:19.
[7] David A. Bednar, "Ye Must Be Born Again," *Ensign*, May 2007.
[8] Eyring, "As a Child," *Ensign*, May 2006.

[9] Tom Jackson, *Tom Jackson's Live Music Method*, 124.
[10] Lynn G. Robbins, "What Manner of Men Ought Ye to Be?" *Ensign*, May 2011.
[11] David O. McKay, as quoted by The Church of Jesus Christ of Latter-day Saints, *Teaching Seminary Preservice Readings Religion 370, 471, and 475*, 61.
[12] James E. Faust, "What I Want My Son to Know Before He Leaves on His Mission," *Ensign*, May 1996.
[13] Doctrine and Covenants 88:40.
[14] Robert D. Hales, "Making Righteous Choices at the Crossroads of Life," *Ensign*, November 1988.
[15] Joseph B. Wirthlin, "The Great Commandment," *Ensign*, November 2007.
[16] Neal A. Maxwell, as quoted by William Baker, "Knowing, Doing, and Being," BYU Devotional, July 25, 2006.
[17] Associated Press, "Steve and Eydie Still Singin' and Swingin'," chronicle.augusta.com/stories/2003/11/26/mus_395673.shtml.
[18] Spencer W. Kimball, "Education for Eternity," BYU Annual Faculty Conference, September 12, 1967.
[19] Dieter F. Uchtdorf, "Your Potential, Your Privilege," *Ensign*, May 2011.
[20] Lawrence M. Berry, "Marriage and the Law of the Harvest," *Liahona*, Aug.-Sep. 1986.
[21] William James, as quoted by Maria Popova, "William James on Habit," brainpickings.org/index.php/2012/09/25/william-james-on-habit/.
[22] 1 Corinthians 1:27.
[23] 1 Corinthians 1:25.
[24] Boyd K. Packer, "The Arts and the Spirit of the Lord," BYU Fireside, February 01, 1976.

Lesson 7:
Revelation

Artist-Disciple Insights

Amber's Story: In Tune

I know that as we are in tune with the Spirit, we can know how to use our talents and artistry. The last few weeks of my mission, I felt inspired to extend a few days so I could participate in a special conference where apostles of the Lord would be present. I was asked to sing "The Lord's Prayer" with the mission president's wife on the violin and another missionary on the piano. We only had a few weeks to practice and limited practice time, but we did our best to prepare and put our trust in the Lord.

We soon found ourselves at the conference and it was time to perform. I stood behind the microphone to sing, took a deep breath and opened my mouth. Everything flowed nicely. I remembered the words that I had translated into Spanish and I hit all of the high notes, which I hadn't done so smoothly in a few of our rehearsals. We all sat down after the performance and I could feel a sweet spirit in the room. I knew that the Lord was pleased with our offering to Him that night.

What surprised me was when the mission president's wife leaned over and asked me in a hurry, "Can you pick out another song? The visiting authority wants us to perform another one." I was shocked, but I reached towards the pew for my hymnal to select another piece. The first song I turned to was "El Amor Del Salvador" ("Our Savior's Love"), which I had performed at the beginning of my mission with the same pianist. I felt the Spirit's confirmation on this song and tried my best to put my trust in the Lord once again.

Not minutes later, one of the General Authorities stood up and told the congregation that according to spiritual promptings he had received, we would be hearing a second song—selected by inspiration—from the missionaries who had performed previously. The three of us stood up, spoke briefly on our plans for the song, and performed. We all took the same pauses and put emphasis in the same areas of the piece. The Spirit of the Lord was guiding us the whole way and I know we wouldn't have been able to perform in this way without His help.

What impressed me about this experience was not that I was asked to sing again, but why I was asked to sing again. After our piece, the General Authority taught us about the power of revelation. It wasn't in anyone's plans to have us sing again, but because it was something the Lord wanted, he was inspired to invite us to do so.

It is the same with our creative works. We can be led, moved and compelled to use our works in the way the Lord would have us do. We may have our own plans, but if we "counsel with the Lord in [all of our] doings, he will direct [us] for good" (Alma 37:37) and help us know how we can best share our talents to bless the lives of others. Then, we are using them in the smartest way and can have the confidence that the Lord is pleased with our efforts, for they truly will be inspired by Him.

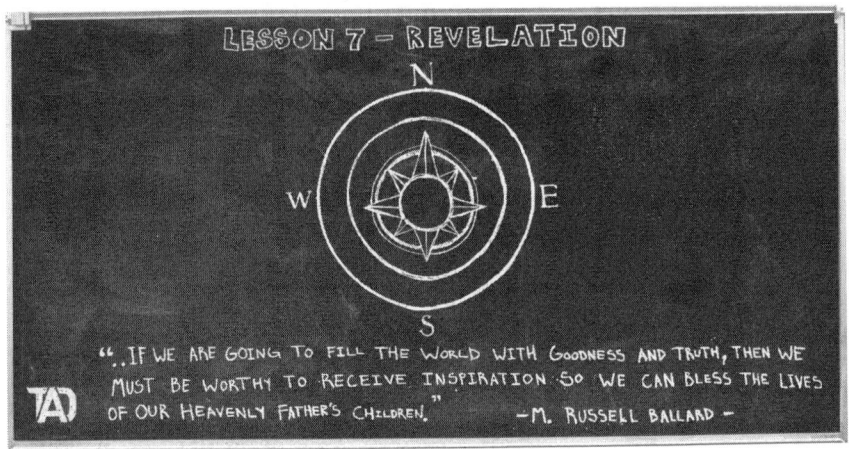

The Most Important Skill

Desire? Check.

Artistic skills? In progress.

Character? Becoming more every day.

Creative work? Looking better and better.

So, what else do I need to know?

Well, first off, Latter-day Saint or not, you cannot do it alone. Nope. Without help from the unseen world, you are pretty much guaranteed failure. Sister Julie B. Beck summed it up pretty well when she said, "The ability to qualify for, receive, and act on personal revelation is the single most important skill that can be acquired in this life."[1]

Going hand in hand with magnification by grace, receiving creative revelation is an ability that pretty much any artist with lasting impact for good has developed. It applies to both Character Ethic and Personality Ethic. It is a skill that will help us overcome the Three Obstacles, produce Transformational Creation, and form the Upstream.

As Elder M. Russell Ballard said, "...If we are going to fill the world with goodness and truth, then we must be worthy to receive inspiration so we can bless the lives of our Heavenly Father's children."[2]

So what does receiving inspiration look like in your life?

A Universal Idea

Really?

It is fascinating to note that most artists admit to some kind of extraterrestrial, external or divine inspiration in their creative work, even if they are not members of the Church of Jesus Christ of Latter-day Saints. Notice the variety of backgrounds in this small sampling of quotations:

> *...every once in a while it seems like the cosmos parts and something great plops into your lap, that's how it was with "Hotel California"...a leased beach house in Malibu... all the doors wide open on a spectacular July day probably in 1975...soaking wet...thinking the world is a wonderful place to be...with an acoustic 12 string...those chords just oozed out.* – Don Felder, The Eagles[3]

> *I immediately feel vibrations that thrill my whole being. These are the Spirit illuminating the soul-power within, and in this exalted state, I see clearly what is obscure in my ordinary moods... Those vibrations assume the forms of distinct mental images, after I have formulated my desire and resolve in regard to what I want—namely, to be inspired so that I can compose something that will uplift and benefit humanity, something of permanent value.* – Brahms[4]

> *The process with me is like a vivid dream...Ideas, clothed in the proper musical setting, stream down upon me. Of course, a*

composer must have mastered the technique of composition, form, theory, harmony, counterpoint, and instrumentation. – Mozart[5]

I don't even know if I can take credit for writing "Cliffs of Dover"...it was just there for me one day...literally written in five minutes...kind of a gift from a higher place that all of us are eligible for. We just have to listen for it and be available to receive it. – Eric Johnson[6]

In the end, we arrive at a kind of model of the artist's world, and that model is that there exist other, higher planes of reality, about which we can prove nothing, but from which arise our lives, our work, and our art. These spheres are trying to communicate with ours... The artist is the servant of that intention, those angels, that Muse... They know they are not the source of the creations they bring into being. They only facilitate. They carry. They are the willing and skilled instruments of the gods and goddesses they serve. – Stephen Pressfield[7]

To me these quotations are significant because they point to a given under which most artists, especially LDS artists, operate: revelation and art are irretrievably enmeshed. The process of creation naturally involves the process of revelation, or clear and specific direction; and inspiration, or small nudges of guidance—both ways we receive from a higher source.

Upstream Through Revelation: Guiding Principles

Before jumping into revelation in the creative process, let's talk about guiding principles for revelation in general that will set the stage for our revelation creatively. These principles include understanding how guidance comes in various forms, its sources, testing revelation, and more. Each of these areas can prove vital to our creativity as artists. Pull out your note-taking gear.

1. Revelation Comes in Various Forms

> *The forms of revelation are limitless. Surely it is not for us to place limits or bounds on the heavens specifying when and how God can communicate his will to us. Common forms of revelation include both the spoken and unspoken word, visitations of angels, dreams, visions, flashes of ideas, impelling impulses, and assurances that come from the Holy Ghost.* – Joseph Fielding McConkie[8]

> *Revelation is communication from God to His children. This guidance comes through various channels according to the needs and circumstances of individuals, families, and the Church as a whole.* – True to the Faith[9]

> *Inspiration is a form and degree of revelation. It is revelation that comes from the still small voice, from the whisperings of the Spirit, from the promptings of the Holy Ghost. All inspiration is revelation.* – Bruce R. McConkie[10]

> *The Holy Ghost communicates important information that we need to guide us in our mortal journey. When it is crisp and clear and essential, it warrants the title of revelation. When it is a series of promptings we often have to guide us step by step to a worthy objective, for the purpose of this message, it is inspiration.* – Richard G. Scott[11]

Got the message? The principle here is that revelation and inspiration come in many different ways. Most often revelation and inspiration come through the Holy Ghost, who also communicates to us in many different ways.[12] So even if your next hit song doesn't come to you in five minutes—like "Cliffs of Dover"—be grateful that you get to participate in the process.

2. Check Your Sources

President Boyd K. Packer taught: "Not all inspiration comes from God."[13]

Why is this important to understand? Because the arts, and our lives, have such power.

As Artist-Disciples, we need to know that there are different spirits in operation in the world— different sources of revelation. The evil one has the power to tap into those channels of revelation and send conflicting signals which can mislead and confuse us. There are promptings from evil sources which are so carefully counterfeited as to deceive even the very elect.[14] Because Artist-Disciples can have such a dramatic effect on the emotions and thoughts and ultimately the lives of the people, it is vitally important to have the power of discernment to recognize what is of God and what is not.

Elder Dallin H. Oaks taught about this principle in a talk he gave on spiritual gifts:

> *Discernment is essential if we are to distinguish between genuine spiritual gifts and the counterfeits Satan seeks to use to deceive men and women and thwart the work of God. The Prophet Joseph Smith said, "Nothing is a greater injury to the children of men than to be under the influence of a false spirit when they think they have the spirit of God." (Teachings, p. 205.)...The Savior warned against false Christs and false prophets who "shall show great signs and wonders, insomuch, that, if possible, they shall deceive the very elect..." (JS-H 1:22) The Apostle John said, "Try the spirits whether they are of God: because many false prophets are gone out into the world."(1 Jn. 4:1)*[15]

This may not seem to be something that most Artist-Disciples deal with on a daily basis, but we need to recognize that not all inspiration is from the same place. We need to understand how to discern between good and evil spirits and the other influences that might seek to inspire us.

For well-meaning and striving Artist-Disciples, this teaching of President Harold B. Lee is comforting: "We get our answer from the source of the power we list to obey."[16]

3. Testing Revelation

Brother Joseph Fielding McConkie gave us a good test to determine if our "revelations" are of God or not:

> *That which professes to be revelation must always be able to give positive answers to such questions as the following:*
>
> 1. *Does it fall within the recipient's stewardship or right to know?*
> 2. *Does it sustain the Lord's anointed and is it in direct compliance with the established order of his kingdom on the earth?*
> 3. *Is it subject to the quiet confirmation of the Spirit?*
> 4. *Does it lead to righteousness?*

He continues by saying:

> *That which comes from God edifies and uplifts. The Spirit of revelation could be described as that influence which makes bad men good and good men better. The light of heaven brings nourishment and strength; where it shines, darkness must flee.*[17]

Elder Dallin H. Oaks also talked about three tests we can apply to revelation to know if it is of God, adding that "True revelation will pass all three of these tests, and spurious revelation (whose source is "of men" or "of devils") will fail at least one of them." The three tests are:

> *1. True revelation will edify the recipient...2. The content of a true revelation must be consistent with the position and responsibilities of the person who receives it...3. True revelation must be consistent with the principles of the gospel as revealed in the scriptures and teachings of the prophets.*[18]

With these tests, a humble heart, and praying for the gift of discernment, we should be able to tell the difference between inspiration from God, from man, or from devils. We can also test the revelation to see how it aligns with our Three Rings.

4. (Not) Being Commanded in All Things

According to Brigham Young, one of our purposes in coming here to this earth is to learn how to be "righteous in the dark," to learn how to be "independent beings."[19]

This applies to our creative work as well. The Lord does not command us in all things. He wants us to learn how to be wise, not slothful, servants.[20] Again, Elder Oaks teaches us about this principle,

> *[A person may have] a strong desire to be led by the Spirit of the Lord but...unwisely extends that desire to the point of wanting to be led in all things. A desire to be led by the Lord is a strength, but it needs to be accompanied by an understanding that our Heavenly Father leaves many decisions for our personal choices. Personal decision making is one of the sources of the growth we are meant to experience in mortality. Persons who try to shift all decision making to the Lord and plead for revelation in every choice will soon find circumstances in which they pray for guidance and don't receive it...*
>
> *We should study things out in our minds, using the reasoning powers our Creator has placed within us. Then we should pray*

> *for guidance and act upon it if we receive it. If we do not receive guidance, we should act upon our best judgment. Persons who persist in seeking revelatory guidance on subjects on which the Lord has not chosen to direct us may concoct an answer out of their own fantasy or bias, or they may even receive an answer through the medium of false revelation.* – Dallin H. Oaks[21]

Many Artist-Disciples want to be guided in every lyric, every brushstroke, and every keystroke. But we need to remember that, in lieu of personal revelation, our "educated conscience"[22] is a good second best. Bruce R. McConkie taught: "Even a righteous person is often left to himself so that he does not at all times enjoy the promptings of revelation and light from the Holy Ghost."[23] This provides us many opportunities to exercise our agency and our creativity and grow through them.

5. They Shall Not Impart…

Alma taught,

> …*It is given unto many to know the mysteries of God; nevertheless they are laid under a strict command that they shall not impart only according to the portion of his word which he doth grant unto the children of men, according to the heed and diligence which they give unto him.*[24]

President Marion G. Romney said, "We'd have more spiritual experiences if we didn't talk so much about them."[25] Sacred experiences are sacred and should not be discussed lightly or with just anybody we feel like sharing them with. Would you trust someone who always told your secrets?

The Lord is willing to give everyone the same knowledge but *they* must qualify for it according to *their* "heed and diligence," not yours. We should be especially cautious about sharing that which is sacred with those who will mock or blaspheme it.[26] Indiscriminately sharing personal revelation decreases the likelihood of receiving more.

Receiving Revelation as We Create

With these guiding principles in mind, let's explore some insights about revelation in the creative process. There are many ways to receive revelation. What follows is meant to be a primer, not an exhaustive treatise. Hopefully it sparks some ideas—even some revelations—for you about how revelation can play a vital role in your Artist-Discipleship. Ponder how these nuggets might apply to your creative work.

1. Call Upon the Lord

I'm often surprised at myself in the creative process. Sometimes I am just like Oliver Cowdery and I take no thought to ask Heavenly Father for guidance.[27] I guess we're in decent company when we forget, because the brother of Jared was guilty of the same thing:

> *And it came to pass at the end of four years that the Lord came again unto the brother of Jared, and stood in a cloud and talked with him. And for the space of three hours did the Lord talk with the brother of Jared, and chastened him because he remembered not to call upon the name of the Lord.*[28]

To avoid a three-hour chastening from the Lord, we need to remember to call upon Him. More importantly, to receive needed guidance in our creative work, we need to remember to call upon Him. No promise is repeated more often in scripture than "ask, and ye shall receive."[29] How often do you call upon the Lord for help in your creative work?

2. *How be it that ye have not written this thing?*

Songwriters are encouraged to always have a "hook book" nearby to record those elusive song ideas when they come along. Why? Because those genius lyrics or that impressive melody might only stay for a short time. Same thing goes for our strokes of magic in pretty much any creative endeavor.

I always have my creative journal with me, and I always keep my study journal close by, especially when I'm working on a project, praying, studying the gospel, attending Church meetings or in any environment where revelation is more likely.

Elder Richard G. Scott taught,

> *Knowledge carefully recorded is knowledge available in time of need. Spiritually sensitive information should be kept in a sacred place that communicates to the Lord how you treasure it. This practice enhances the likelihood of your receiving further light.*[30]

Record-keeping is important to the Lord. When the Savior learned that what He had told His servant Samuel had not been written, he "commanded that it should be written; therefore it was written as he commanded."[31] Elsewhere He urged the Church, "Behold, there shall be a record kept among you."[32]

From a practical and spiritual standpoint, writing and recording the light we receive should be important to Artist-Disciples as well. We might not think we could ever forget those precious morsels of inspiration it, but if we don't record them, we will lose them. The amazing thing is that the Lord promises that those who receive His lines and precepts will receive more[33] and more light and that their light will grow brighter and brighter until the perfect day.[34]

3. Is there more I should know?

Consider the process shared by Elder Scott when he began to receive personal revelation in the middle of a church meeting:

> *...Strong impressions began to flow to me...I wrote them down. The message included specific counsel on how to become more effective as an instrument in the hands of the Lord. I received such an outpouring of impressions that were so personal that I felt it was not appropriate to record them in the midst of a Sunday School class. I sought a more private location, where I continued to write the feelings that flooded into my mind and heart as faithfully as possible.*
>
> *After each powerful impression was recorded, I pondered the feelings I had received to determine if I had accurately expressed them in writing. As a result, I made a few minor changes to what had been written. Then I studied their meaning and application in my own life. Subsequently I prayed, reviewing with the Lord what I thought I had been taught by the Spirit. When a feeling of peace came, I thanked Him for the guidance given. I was then impressed to ask, "Was there yet more to be given?"*

How often have you asked this question in the middle of your creative work? Perhaps not as often as would be best. Look at what happened because Elder Scott continued to ask:

> *I received further impressions, and the process of writing down the impressions, pondering, and praying for confirmation was repeated. Again I was prompted to ask, "Is there more I should know?" And there was. When that last, most sacred experience was concluded, I had received some of the most precious, specific, personal direction one could hope to obtain in this life. Had I not responded to the first impressions and recorded them, I would not have received the last, most precious guidance.*[35]

If we want to receive counsel on how to become "more effective as an instrument in the hands of the Lord," then we must keep asking. We need not settle for breadcrumbs when God is willing to give us the loaf.

4. While He May Be Found

The prophet Isaiah counseled, "Seek ye the Lord while he may be found, call ye upon him while he is near:"[36] And where is the Lord to be found?

> *...And, behold, the Lord passed by, and a great and strong wind rent the mountains, and brake in pieces the rocks before the Lord; but the Lord was not in the wind: and after the wind an earthquake; but the Lord was not in the earthquake: And after the earthquake a fire; but the Lord was not in the fire: and after the fire a still small voice.*[37]

President Boyd K. Packer taught that "reverence invites revelation."[38] President Henry B. Eyring said, "Only when my heart has been still and quiet, in submission like a little child, has the Spirit been clearly audible to my heart and mind."[39] Sometimes it is necessary to be still and know that He is God.[40] We don't necessarily have to go up to a high mountain, to the temple, out in nature, or in our closets to find God, although these things can help. The Lord can be found almost anywhere as long as we are still enough.

5. Be Reconciled

This experience of the Prophet Joseph Smith as told by David Whitmer has always inspired me:

> *One morning when he was getting ready to continue the translation, something went wrong about the house and he was*

> *put out about it. Something that Emma, his wife, had done. Oliver and I went upstairs, and Joseph came up soon after to continue the translation, but he could not do anything. He could not translate a single syllable. He went down stairs, out into the orchard and made supplication to the Lord; was gone about an hour—came back to the house, asked Emma's forgiveness and then came up stairs where we were and the translation went on all right. He could do nothing save he was humble and faithful.*[41]

Martin Harris had a similar experience as he sought to be one of the three special witnesses to the gold plates. It was only after reconciling himself to God that he was privileged to see the plates.[42] The Savior taught,

> *Therefore if thou bring thy gift to the altar, and there rememberest that thy brother hath ought against thee; Leave there thy gift before the altar, and go thy way; first be reconciled to thy brother, and then come and offer thy gift.*[43]

I've found this principle to be true as I've tried to perform my offering. Nothing stops the spirit of revelation faster than the spirit of contention or having an outstanding account with the Lord or any of His children.

6. Rely upon the things which are written

In the eighteenth section of the Doctrine and Covenants, the Lord instructed Oliver Cowdery:

> *Behold, I have manifested unto you, by my Spirit in many instances, that the things which you have written are true; wherefore you know that they are true. And if you know that they are true, behold, <u>I give unto you a commandment, that you rely upon the things which are written;</u>*[44]

Elder Robert D. Hales taught, "...when we want to speak to God, we pray. And when we want Him to speak to us, we search the scriptures; for His words are spoken through His prophets. He will then teach us as we listen to the promptings of the Holy Spirit."[45] I have found many times that studying the scriptures can be the key to unlocking the power of revelation. I've also found that, when praying for new revelation, the Lord will often just refer me back to previous personal revelation He's already given. This goes for artistry as well as every other area of my life.

7. 10% Inspiration, 90% Perspiration

Joseph Smith taught,

> *A person may profit by noticing the first intimation of the spirit of revelation; for instance, when you feel pure intelligence flowing into you, it may give you sudden strokes of ideas, so that by noticing it, you may find it fulfilled the same day or soon...thus by learning the Spirit of God and understanding it, you may grow into the principle of revelation, until you become perfect in Christ Jesus.*[46]

Sometimes the "first intimation" is all I seem to get. I have "sudden strokes of ideas" but then I am left to work things out for myself. It does no good to wait around for the Muse to land on me again and give me the next step. I have found that further inspiration comes as I work.

Chuck Close, an artist known for his larger-than-life portraits, said that "Inspiration is for amateurs. Inspiration is in the work."[47] He went on to say that folks waiting around for "inspiration" are waiting for nothing.

Cheryl Lant, former General Primary President said, "Our faith has to be in motion for the Lord's blessings to come. We must pray as if everything depends on the Lord, and then get up and work as if everything depends on us."[48]

Sometimes, however, rather than a flash of inspiration, I receive a flood of inspiration. I have learned to be very grateful for these tender moments, but I don't count on them to come every day. As I've worked through the dark patches, I've learned that light comes when I need it most. We should remember that God is more concerned with the development of us as creators than He is with the development of our creations. If He cared more about the projects we're working on, He'd just create them Himself.

8. "Sydney is not used to it..."

Elder Philo Dibble did not see the vision of the three degrees of Celestial glory, recorded in Doctrine and Covenants Section 76, but he did observe the Prophet and Sydney Rigdon as they experienced the vision. After the vision was over, Elder Dibble recorded, "Joseph sat firmly and calmly all the time in the midst of a magnificent glory, but Sidney sat limp and pale, apparently as limber as a rag, observing which, Joseph remarked, smilingly, 'Sidney is not used to it as I am.'"[49]

This description of Sydney Rigdon sounds somewhat similar to how Joseph himself felt after his night of visitations from the angel Moroni: "...I found my strength so exhausted as to render me entirely unable."[50]

General Tom Thumb, a little person who achieved fame as a circus performer under P.T. Barnum, once interviewed Brigham Young and apparently indicated to President Young that there were some things he couldn't understand about Mormonism. President Young reportedly responded: "Don't worry, when I was your size I didn't understand [them] either."[51]

We can grow into the principle of revelation. We can become more used to it and develop spiritual stamina and stature. Over time and with practice, our capacity will increase. President Heber J. Grant said,

> *That which we persist in doing becomes easier for us to do; not that the nature of the thing is changed, but that our power to do is increased.*[52]

9. Quickening

Joseph Smith revealed this truth about the process of receiving revelation:

> *All things whatsoever God in his infinite wisdom has seen fit and proper to reveal to us, while we are dwelling in mortality, in regard to our mortal bodies, are revealed to us in the abstract, and independent of affinity of this mortal tabernacle, but are revealed to our spirits precisely as though we had no bodies at all; and those revelations which will save our spirits will save our bodies. God reveals them to us in view of no eternal dissolution of the body, or tabernacle.*[53]

Commenting on the above quotation from the Prophet, President Packer said,

> *Should an angel appear and converse with you, neither you nor he would be confined to corporeal sight or sound in order to communicate. For there is that spiritual process, described by the Prophet Joseph Smith, by which pure intelligence can flow into our minds and we can know what we need to know without either the drudgery of study or the passage of time, for it is revelation.*[54]

The process of learning by revelation is different than the process of learning in the classroom. We can learn a semester's worth of information in seconds by the power of the Spirit. But don't be surprised if you have a hard time communicating what you've learned.

> *The gospel of the Son of God...is from eternity to eternity. When the vision of the mind is opened, you can see a great portion of it, but you see it comparatively as a speaker sees the faces of a congregation. To look at, and talk to each individual separately, and thinking to become fully acquainted with them, only to spend five minutes with each would consume too much time, it could not easily be done. So it is with the visions of eternity; we can see and understand, but it is difficult to tell.* – Brigham Young[55]

Like trying to explain how salt tastes, it is difficult to explain "in words alone everything you know spiritually."[56]

Developing Your Personal Vision

As we come to understand the process of revelation in our lives and creative work, we gain a better understanding of our work as an Artist-Disciple and our place in the prophetic vision of the Latter-day Saints we explored in Lesson 1. Whether your audience is thirty or 30 million, you can be an individual piece in creating what the prophets have seen of what the world is to become.

What is your cellophane?

A story is told of a bunch of flies that were put in a clear glass jar with cellophane on top. The flies learned that they could not fly through the apparent opening, and even when the cellophane was removed they did not attempt to escape the jar. Unfortunately, that is too often the story of those who have been given gifts and talents to create good and beautiful things.

One of the most amazing benefits of personal revelation in our artistic work is that it helps us see beyond the limitations we place upon ourselves and to a realm of possibility beyond ourselves. The world, and especially the adversary, influences you and me to think small and stay small. Satan wants us to believe that there are invisible ceilings between us and our potential because that is his fate. Like those flies, he is able to see a *view* of his and our potential, but because of his choice to rebel against God, he is not able to obtain it himself. As a result, he wants to limit our *vision* so that we never attain it either. He wants us to become discouraged by failure and invisible ceilings and give up.

Glorious Views of Happiness

Revelation is a key to understanding what our true potential is and can be. One of the Prophet Joseph's greatest challenges was to get the Saints to see the vision he had. The Lord has the same challenge. He sees us not as we now are, but as we have the power to become. If we can rend the veil of unbelief[57] and see with an "eye of faith,"[58] we can break through invisible ceilings and be the means of doing much good in this generation.[59] Even more than that, we will then be on the path toward receiving some of the greatest happiness we have ever known.

A Formula for Artist-Disciples...and Many Others

In what ways will these principles of revelation impact your creative process? Hopefully they have opened your eyes, as they have mine, to even more possibilities.

I knew a wise man, one of my mentors, who shared with me a formula for transforming things in this world, overcoming the Three

Obstacles, and more fully living within our Rings and Identities. It went something like this:

1. Count the cost and see if you have what it takes.
2. Then go to the Lord and learn *by revelation* what it means to seek the Kingdom of God first.
3. Then go out into the world and seek all the knowledge the world has to offer without compromising your standards.
4. Overcome the world by knowledge.
5. And the Lord will show you what belongs to Zion.

If you will take your current projects through this process, as well as those you see in the future, you will find your capacity and vision increasing. President Packer said,

> *The ideal, of course, is for one with a gift to train and develop it to the highest possibility, including a sense of spiritual propriety. No artist in the Church who desires unselfishly to extend our heritage need sacrifice his career or an avocation, nor need he neglect his gift as only a hobby. He can meet the world and "best" it, and not be the loser. In the end, what appears to be such sacrifice will have been but a test.*[60]

Building Zion

Are you energized at the prospect of overcoming the world—of besting it? Are you fascinated by the line, "And the Lord will show you what belongs to Zion"? To me, that seems to be at least part of the key to overcoming the world.

Nephi, when he was commanded to build a boat, "...did not work the timbers after the manner which was learned by men, neither did [he] build the ship after the manner of men; but [he] did build it after the manner which the Lord had shown unto [him]; wherefore it was not after the manner of men"[61]

I believe that the Lord is willing and wanting to give us guidance in all the creative work we do to further His Kingdom. I believe He will show us more excellent ways to do that work that will not be "after the manner of men" or "after the rudiments of the world."[62]

Receiving and acting on revelation, like any skill, takes effort. We should not expect it to be instantaneous or easy all of the time. Elder David A. Bednar said that Nephi "…did not learn how to build a ship of curious workmanship all at one time; rather, he was shown by the Lord 'from time to time after what manner [he] should work the timbers of the ship' (1 Nephi 18:1)."[63] But he was shown! And so will we be shown.

We end, as we began, with words from Sister Julie Beck on revelation, who said "We can do the work of the Lord in His way when we seek, receive, and act on personal revelation. Without personal revelation, we cannot succeed. If we heed personal revelation, we cannot fail."[64]

Is it time for you to be shown what belongs to Zion in your creative work?

Questions and Action Items:

1. In what ways can you access the power of revelation in your creative work today?

2. Take a moment to review revelation you have already received, by reading records you have kept or asking the Spirit to bring all things to your remembrance. How can you better implement this revelation into your Artist-Discipleship?

3. How can you use your study journal/idea book to maximize the power of inspiration and revelation in your life?

4. Consider the "Formula" for Artist-Disciples described above. What "belongs to Zion" in your life?

Chapter Summary

- The most important skill you can acquire in this life is the ability to qualify for, receive and act on personal revelation.
- Because qualifying for, receiving and acting on personal revelation is a skill and a gift that can be received and developed, there are many principles and guidelines that can help us. Many of these concepts are included in this chapter.
- We can overcome the world and be shown what belongs to Zion.
- Developing the ability to receive personal revelation will quicken your creativity, hasten your personal progress and amplify all of your work.

[1] Julie B. Beck, "And Upon the Handmaids in Those Days I Will Pour Out My Spirit," *Ensign,* May 2010.
[2] M. Russell Ballard, "Filling the World with Goodness and Truth," *Ensign,* July 1996.
[3] Don Felder, guitarworld.com/100-greatest-guitar-solos-no-8-hotel-california-don-felder-joe-walsh.
[4] David Glen Hatch, *Praiseworthy Music and Spiritual Moments,* 56.
[5] Wolfgang Amadeus Mozart, walterrobinsmusic.com/vivid-dream-part-2.html.
[6] Eric Johnson, guitarworld.com/100-greatest-guitar-solos-no-17-cliffs-dover-eric-johnson.
[7] Stephen Pressfield, *The War of Art: Break Through the Blocks and Win Your Inner Creative Battles,* 163.
[8] Joseph Fielding McConkie, *Seeking the Spirit,* 53.
[9] The Church of Jesus Christ of Latter-day Saints, *True to the Faith,* 140.
[10] Bruce R. McConkie, *Mormon Doctrine,* 383.
[11] Richard G. Scott, "How to Obtain Revelation and Inspiration for Your Personal Life," *Ensign,* May 2012.
[12] For an extensive list of how the Holy Ghost communicates with us, see *Preach My Gospel,* 96-99.
[13] Boyd K. Packer, as quoted by Sally T. Taylor, "The Holy Ghost: Our Infallible Guide," BYU Devotional, November 05, 1996.
[14] Matthew 24:24.
[15] Dallin H. Oaks, "Spiritual Gifts," *Ensign,* September 1986.
[16] Harold B. Lee, "Stories from the General Authorities: President Harold B. Lee," *New Era,* March 1973.
[17] Joseph Fielding McConkie, *Seeking the Spirit,* 96.
[18] Dallin H. Oaks, "Reason and Revelation," 13-15.
[19] Brigham Young, *Brigham Young's Office Journal, January 28, 1857,* Archives of The Church of Jesus Christ of Latter-day Saints.
[20] D&C 58:26.
[21] Dallin H. Oaks, as quoted by The Church of Jesus Christ of Latter-day Saints, *Preach My Gospel,* 101.
[22] Steven R. Covey, "An Educated Conscience," BYU Devotional, May 27, 1975.
[23] Bruce R. McConkie, *Doctrinal New Testament Commentary Vol. II,* 107.
[24] Alma 12:9.
[25] Marion G. Romney, as quoted by Neal A. Maxwell, "Becoming a Disciple," *Ensign,* June 1996.
[26] Matthew 7:6.
[27] Doctrine and Covenants 9:7-9.
[28] Ether 2:14.
[29] Doctrine and Covenants 4:7.

30 Richard G. Scott, "Acquiring Spiritual Knowledge," *Ensign*, November 1993.
31 3 Nephi 24:9-13.
32 Doctrine and Covenants 21:1.
33 2 Nephi 28:30.
34 Doctrine and Covenants 50:24.
35 Richard G. Scott, "To Acquire Spiritual Guidance," *Ensign*, November 2009.
36 Isaiah 55:6.
37 1 Kings 19:11-12.
38 Boyd K. Packer, "Reverence Invites Revelation," *Ensign*, November 1991.
39 Henry B. Eyring, "As a Child," *Ensign*, May 2006.
40 Psalms 46:10.
41 David Whitmer, as quoted by Dallin H. Oaks, "Two Lines of Communication," *Ensign*, November 2010.
42 Doctrine and Covenants 5, 32.
43 Matthew 5:23-24.
44 Doctrine and Covenants 18:2-3, emphasis added.
45 Robert D. Hales, "Holy Scriptures: The Power of God unto Our Salvation," *Ensign*, November 2006.
46 Joseph Smith, *History of the Church*, 3:381.
47 Chuck Close, http://www.goodreads.com/author/quotes/166434.Chuck_Close.
48 Cheryl Lant, "He Does Not Take Counsel From His Fears," BYU Women's Conference, May 4, 2007.
49 Philo Dibble, as quoted by Joseph Fielding McConkie, *Seeking the Spirit*, 39-40.
50 Joseph Smith—History 1:48.
51 McConkie, *Seeking the Spirit*, 72.
52 Heber J. Grant, *Teachings of Presidents of the Church: Heber J. Grant*, 33.
53 Joseph Smith, as quoted by Truman G. Madsen, "On How We Know," BYU Devotional, September 20, 1994.
54 Boyd K. Packer, "The Candle of the Lord," *Ensign*, January 1983.
55 Brigham Young, *Teachings of Presidents of the Church: Brigham Young*, 12.
56 Packer, "The Candle of the Lord," *Ensign*, January 1983.
57 Ether 4:15.
58 Alma 5:15; Alma 32:40; Ether 12:19.
59 Doctrine and Covenants 11:8.
60 Boyd K. Packer, "The Arts and the Spirit of the Lord," BYU Fireside, February 01, 1976.
61 1 Nephi 18:2.
62 Colossians 2:8.
63 David A. Bednar, "Line Upon Line, Precept Upon Precept," *New Era*, 4.
64 Julie B. Beck, "Fulfilling the Purpose of Relief Society," *Ensign*, November 2008.

Section III: Transformational Creation

Lesson 8:
Transformational Creation

Artist-Disciple Insights

Arian's Story: Creating with the Creator

I learned a lot while making my first CD, but the most important thing that came from the process was how I changed and grew personally. When the idea came to me to record a CD, it terrified me and I immediately pushed the thought away: "Who am I to record an album? There are so many who could do it so much better than me."

As time went by and the idea wouldn't leave me alone, I gradually realized that this was something the Lord wanted me to do and that no one else could do it for me—no one else would choose the same pieces for the same reasons, or express them exactly the way I would. I needed the growth of accepting myself and what I could offer others through the talents He gave me. I needed to experience the change of priorities from, "What will others think of this?" to "How can I use what God has given me to bless those who hear this? How can I create this in a way that the Spirit is in it?" I learned to take the terrifying spotlight off myself and turn it to the creation itself.

I prayed my way through every step of the project, and I had a really amazing experience one night as I lay in bed. I was wide awake and the pieces I'd been practicing for the recording started playing vividly in my mind. I heard every note in the correct key from start to finish, and then the next song began, in its new key, from start to finish. After the third or fourth song, I realized what was happening: the order of the pieces was being given to me. It was a revelatory experience like I'd never had before. It was also getting really late and I knew I needed to get some sleep, so I tried to fast-forward through each piece to the end, so I could hear which song came next. It worked.

And then something very interesting happened. One of the pieces I'd planned to record never showed up. But a different piece I'd never considered for this album did. I knew it was being given to me by the Spirit. So I turned my lamp on, jotted down the order, and then was able to fall asleep. That was one of the ways the Lord directed my creation once I learned to take myself out of it and let it be His.

Now when people tell me what they think of my album, regardless of their faith, almost without exception each person describes how it makes them feel. They are referring to the Spirit, whether they know that's what it is or not. That's how I measure its success—not by how others see me as a musician, but by how it makes them feel. I am so grateful I learned this in the process. It is an amazing experience to be able to create with the Creator.

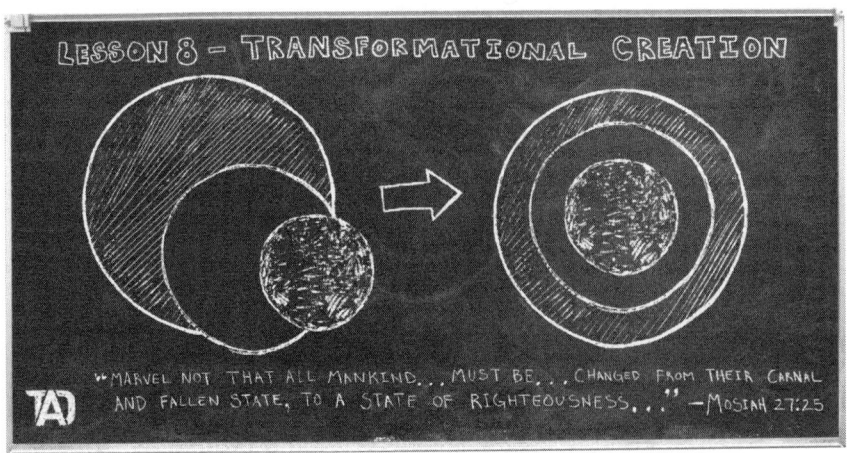

Upstream to Transformation

In the Upstream diagram Lesson 3, what did the pool at the end of the river represent?

Weren't expecting a pop quiz, were you?

I will give you a hint: all art and media have an effect, to a large or small degree, on the lives, thoughts, emotions, attitudes, culture, and eventually laws of those who are exposed to them.

The answer to our quiz, of course, is that these things are represented by the pool at the end of the river.

Our goal in forming the Upstream is to help ensure that the lives, thoughts, emotions, attitudes, culture, and eventually laws of our own families, community, nation and eventually the world are filled with goodness and truth and the path that leads to true happiness.

In the past four lessons, we have discussed some of the key principles that set the Upstream apart from the Mainstream, such as our Identities as disciples and children of God, being founded on Christ, becoming as well as creating, and seeking revelation in our creative process. Now we move into a further discussion of the ultimate goal of the Upstream: transforming lives.

What does "Transformational" mean?

In Lesson 5 we learned:

- Transformational Creation is creation intended to transform.
- Transformational Creation is one of the three liberating characteristics of Christocentric creation and, as such, it too is Christ-centered.
- Transformational Creation is closely associated with the leader-servant mentality. It is not selfish but seeks the "benefit of the world."[1]
- Transformational Creation is focused on transforming people. It is focused, at least in some way, on leading men and women along the eternal progression continuum (the EPC) from telestial to terrestrial to celestial—from bad to good and on, changing human nature.
- Transformational Creation is very much about motives—the orientation of your heart and your purpose for creating.
- Transformational Creation does not have to be celestial (i.e. of the gospel, spiritual or inspirational artistic genre; *directly* teaching gospel principles) to be transformational. You can teach people the gospel without them knowing they're being taught the gospel.
- Transformational Creation is purpose-driven. It is immersed in higher purpose and it is often surrounded in strategy.

I'll include a few definitional additives here as well to give shape to the rest of our discussion.

trans·for·ma·tion: 1. a. The act or an instance of transforming. b. The state of being transformed. 2. A marked change, as in appearance or character, <u>usually for the better</u>.²

trans·form: 1. To change markedly the appearance or form of. 2. To change the <u>nature</u>, function, or condition of; <u>convert</u>.³

cre·a·tion: 1. a. The act of creating. b. The fact or state of having been created....5. An original product of human invention or artistic imagination.⁴

cre·ate: 1. To cause to exist; bring into being....2. To give rise to; produce:...4. To produce through artistic or imaginative effort.⁵

With this review and these definitions as a foundation, let's drill down.

People Want to Be Transformed

Live concert producer Tom Jackson said that people go to a concert, a show, a performance (or for our purposes, any type of interaction with the arts) for three reasons:

1. To be captured and engaged
2. To experience moments
3. To be transformed; to be changed[6]

Music coach Cari Cole also says that fans listen to your music or go to your performance to be changed, to escape from their reality to yours, to lift or change their emotional state.[7] One writer said that people read books because "...you find yourself in a book."[8] Others talk about other factors like community, fun, the social element, the experience, etc. Whatever the language, the deep-down internal motive is still the same—people want to be transformed.

By and large, most people possess an innate tugging for progression. We came to this earth to become like our Father in Heaven, and our desire to progress is part of our nature. As the prophet Nephi said, "...men are, that they might have joy."⁹ In other words, men and women exist to have joy. If we are not experiencing joy, we naturally seek to find it. Our desire to progress is intimately connected with our nature to find joy.

What do *you* want?

I was intrigued when I did a little Internet search using the key phrase, "What do people want out of life?" Some of the answers were ridiculously shallow, but others were meaningful. One site listed categories such as spirituality, meaningful life, happiness, peace of mind, productivity, self-acceptance and confidence, meaningful work. All of these categories and the bullet points listed under them pointed to people's innate desire for joy, for progression, for transformation.

In 1975 and again in 1993, the Church conducted a survey polling new converts and asking them the question, "What initially interested you in the Church?" The top three answers were:

1. The feeling of closeness to God, which they wanted and witnessed in the lives of their LDS friends.
2. The desire for true happiness and a sense of peace, which they wanted and witnessed in their LDS friends.
3. A better sense of purpose and direction, which they wanted and observed in the lives of their LDS friends.¹⁰

The word that stands out to me in these responses is "wanted." The converts "wanted" something better. When people engage in an artistic experience (i.e. listen to a CD, go to a concert, read a book, watch a movie, study a painting, etc.), they come to the experience wanting to somehow be changed—to have more joy.

This places you as an Artist-Disciple in a very unique position. People *want* you to be the one who captures and engages them. They *want* you to be the one who transforms them. Again, people have different ideas about how to "have joy." Some seek for "happiness in doing iniquity."[11] But this is where you come in. As an Artist-Disciple you know that "wickedness never was happiness."[12] You also know how to lead people to true happiness. You are in the privileged position of being able to transform people for the better.

"I have a feeling"

Did you notice the story shared by Artist-Disciple Arian just before this chapter? Arian is practicing many of the traits of Transformational Creation, and we will refer to her throughout this discussion. Consider her words: "When people tell me what they think of my album, regardless of their faith, almost without exception, each person describes how it makes them feel…" In other words, "feeling" is a key component of Transformational Creation, and this is just one example.

Before we talk about "how" to transform people through our creations, we need to talk a little more about "what" Transformational Creation is. Listed below are some more characteristics to add to what we reviewed at the beginning of today's lesson. They will help us understand how we can approach our creative work with a Transformational Creation mindset.

Transformational Creation…

Possesses many of the attributes of charity. Ponder how these statements on charity might apply to your creative work and your creations: "And charity suffereth long, and is kind, and envieth not, and is not puffed up, seeketh not her own, is not easily provoked, thinketh no evil, and rejoiceth not in iniquity but rejoiceth in the truth, beareth all things, believeth all things, hopeth all things, endureth all things."[13] In many ways, as Arian said, it "take[s] the terrifying spotlight off [ourselves] and turn[s] it to the creation itself."

Preaches repentance without necessarily preaching. Here's another review my family's show received on TripAdvisor.com: "Over the past few months I have attended The Brett's show over 10 times, not because I'm a 'groupie' but because of the way I feel at the show. They provide an uplifting and inspiring experience…Every show makes me want to be better. A better daughter. A better sister. A better friend. A better neighbor and citizen of this great country."[14]

This person experienced a "change of mind and heart that [gave]…a fresh view about God, about [herself]], and about the world," which is how the booklet "True to the Faith" describes repentance.[15] We might not be standing on a wall with arrows, stones and other projectiles being hurled at us, but any time people experience these types of changes, we have been preaching repentance.

Is not self-indulgent. I once went to the concert of an artist who was an expert guitarist and vocalist. He was very, very good. Unfortunately, to me he seemed to get into the music so much that he excluded his audience, including myself, sitting on the front row. Worse, he seemed to get into himself so much that it was a real turn-off to those of us there. He was good enough to keep people's attention, but I think he's missing out on the power he could have if he cared more about his fans and their experience than himself.

Is purpose <u>and</u> mission-driven. Transformational Creation aligns with an Artist-Disciple's purpose (to become like Christ) and his or her personal mission or offering. Additionally, creation with a transformational nature tends to have a purpose within an artist's overall strategy. We'll discuss that a little bit more in a page or two.

Is "For the Strength of Youth" worthy. This is a given. Transformational Creation cannot violate standards and become a good standard to the nations at the same time.

Seeks to connect with people. Since the purpose of Transformational Creation is to transform people, it makes sense that the artist would have people in mind during its creation. People are the ends, not the means. Additionally, it's important for Artist-Disciples themselves to seek to connect with people. If audiences feel transformation in your work, they'll want to connect with you as a creator. You might create or perform for the masses, but you'll find a lot of celestial work to be done with "the one" after the show, on your Facebook page, or backstage. Your creation and conversation can help lead people to Christ.

Is NOT necessarily avant-garde. A friend and I once prayerfully wrote a simple children's song for a multi-ward Primary camp here in our area. We did our best under the circumstances, but to us the lyrics seemed cheesy, the music track sounded tacky, and the melody could have been much more interesting. Technically, it was anything but a masterpiece. But we've received more positive feedback on this song than almost anything else we have done. The tune and lyrics fit the taste of the children who were our audience. Parents and leaders texted us, called us, stopped us in the hallway to tell us how much they felt the Spirit as the children sang the song. Our efforts as we learned our craft were magnified by the Spirit; and although the song wasn't cutting edge, it touched souls and changed hearts. It was more transformational than a lot of the "cutting edge" stuff we'd tried to create before. Instead of making the avant-garde our highest priority, as so many artists are tempted to do, we experienced Transformational Creation by combining it with the other elements of discipleship.

Seeks to be timeless and enduring. The great artistic creations of history have stood the test of time and continue to teach and inspire people even though the artist has long since passed. Transformational

Creation seeks to be timeless and enduring. It is one way for the artist to continue his or her mission/offering after he or she passes away.

Transformational Creation is the type of creation that will form the Upstream. This means its quality will be stellar enough to break through the Mainstream and influence the culture and laws of society in positive, Kingdom-building ways. The key words here are positive and Kingdom-building.

In contrast...

Like everything else, Transformational Creation has its opposite. I like to call this Destructive Creation. Transformational Creation changes people for the better; Destructive Creation changes people for the worse. It destroys, not builds. It is a "disturber and an annoyer" of the Lord's work.

Many artists throughout history—intentionally or unintentionally—have had negative effects on the spiritual and moral fiber of society. Transformational Creation is a facilitator for the Lord's work. When you understand principles of Transformational Creation, you can hone your abilities to transform the world for the better. All creation has an effect on the world. Which would you rather do—create uplifting and building art which spans the ages, or destroy the society in which you live by chipping away at its moral framework?

What does it take?

To produce Transformational Creation, it takes everything we've talked about in this book so far:

1. The Vision – Development of and commitment to personal and prophetic vision.

2. The Power – Righteous use of artistic power and influence
3. The Problem – Overcoming sin and worldliness, isolation and mediocrity.
4. The Foundation – Commitment to identity, purpose, callings, and mission.
5. The Lodestar – Making Christ the lodestar of all your artistic endeavors.
6. The X Factor – The CE/PE Balance plus magnification by grace.
7. Revelation – Acquisition of the skill of seeking, receiving and acting on personal revelation.

In this lesson, I would also like to suggest two more ingredients that you will almost certainly need as you seek to produce Transformational Creation:

1. Purpose, Goals, Strategy

Although it is possible to transform without them, think how much more can be done with strategy, goals, and purpose. Planning opens the doors to many more opportunities to influence your audiences for the better. If you are an artist like me who makes a living producing a non-celestial art form or who is not producing celestial work all of the time, this is especially helpful to understand. May I go beyond what we have discussed in previous lessons and illustrate using my original music?

Popular, yet clean

I write music in the pop/R&B genre. My goal is to bring positive and clean messages to the mainstream market wrapped in fresh and innovative pop/R&B sounds. My strategy and overall purpose is to bring people to Christ, prepare the world for the Second Coming, and build up the Kingdom of God. So when I write a song, I keep my purpose, goals, and strategy in mind. I try to purposely build the songs so they will fit in some way into that strategy.

For instance, I might write a dance song that seemingly has nothing to do with the gospel, but it does communicate that good clean fun can be had at a dance. The song is one piece in my repertoire and it has a purpose. It might become the hit that catapults me into fame and influence, but it is just one song. I have other songs that serve other purposes within my album or my live performances. All in all, though, they work synergistically to achieve the overall strategy of bringing souls to Christ. I figure if I can capture people and attract them to me, then I have a better chance of leading them to Christ.

Be careful

A quick word of caution about strategy here. I've been very transparent with mine for the purposes of illustration. But your strategy isn't necessarily something you want to wear on your sleeve. You don't want people walking up to you and saying, "Oh, you're strategy's showing."

Successful artists have a plan and their success is orchestrated. It carries into their systems and structures, their business, and all the details of their work. For now the principle is this—even if it is not directly celestial work, your creation can ultimately have celestial impact as you strategically create with a transformational mentality.

2. *Effort and Time*

It takes time. And effort. And an investment from yourself. There's significance in the language from the 13th Article of Faith: "We *seek* after these things..." [16] The virtuous, the lovely, that which is of good report and praiseworthy often take more seeking to find than their worldly counterparts.

Why do I say this? Because clean takes a different kind of investment than dirty. It's easy to get a cheap laugh by using profanity. It's easy to get a cheap thrill by showing some skin. It is often hard work to create clean at the level of excellence required to compete. Artist-Disciples know this and allow for the time it will take to produce appealing clean.

No hokiness allowed

How can we, like our friend Arian, who "prayed [her] way through every step of the project," not settle for the coarseness of the world? How can we create innovative methods of expression that will ultimately be more popular than the cookie-cutter crudeness so pervasive in the arts and entertainment today?

By being willing to take the necessary time and effort to develop such innovative expression. Without this, our art will most likely end up being cheesy or hokey. Transformational Creation is not hokey. It is excellent and it is appealing because it accords with the deepest within us. It accords with truth. As Artist-Disciples, we must be vigilant enough in pursuing the path of truth and avoid taking the path of least resistance. If we do this, we have a much better chance of creating something worthy of who we are meant to be.

Transformational Creators

Have you ever watched those cooking shows on television? I've seen a few, and I can guarantee you that I could use exactly the same recipe as those professional cooks and come up with a vastly different result. Why? Because I am not Chef Boyardee. I am not Rachael Ray. The recipe comes to life because of the cook.

Transformational Creation works much the same way. It is the unique set of attributes and skills—who you are—that you bring to the creative table that ultimately gives your creation transformational appeal. It is what Dr. Suzuki of the Suzuki Method, calls your "voice of life." We're back to becoming, the X factor, to the CE/PE Balance. In the end, Transformational Creation is an extension of the creator. As you focus on who you are becoming, many of the ingredients we've discussed today will naturally come along and fall into place within your creation.

Think back to Arian for a moment. She said, "I learned a lot while making my first CD, but the most important thing that came from the process was how I changed and grew personally…the Lord directed my creation once I learned to take myself out of it and let it be His." There is a vital need for Transformational Creation in our world today. But more than that, there is a need for Transformational *Creators*.

Out of the Same Mouth

Transformational Creation comes from Artist-Disciples who are striving to do good and to *be* good. Transformational Creators are not only striving to transform; they are striving to be transformed themselves.

There is good and bad in every genre and in every artist. I have an intense respect for Michael Jackson's creative work and abilities. I believe he was—at his core—a good person. Yet some of his creations were destructive. "Man in the Mirror" is an inspiring song. "Dirty Diana" is not. "Out of the same mouth proceedeth blessing and cursing…these things ought not so to be."[17] This duality can deceive audiences.

You'll remember how Alma chastened his son Corianton when Corianton had undermined the missionary work they had been sent to do among the Zoramites:

> *...Behold, O my son, how great iniquity ye brought upon the Zoramites; for when they saw your conduct they would not believe my words.*[18]

We will make the biggest difference in the world as we strive to both produce Transformational Creation and *be* Transformational Creators.

Heavenly Father – The Ultimate Transformational Creator

> *For behold, this is my work and my glory – to bring to pass the immortality and eternal life of man.*[19]

Our Heavenly Father's work is transformational. His goal is to transform us into celestial beings. He has the same objective for all of His creations. His motive is love. It is to serve us. Everything He does is for people. He created the earth that it should be inhabited by us[20] and to provide a place for us to prove ourselves and become more like Him.[21] When we talk about Kingdom-building we need to realize that, for Him, it is not architectural—although there are some beautiful buildings and landscapes in His kingdom. For Him, Kingdom-building is people-building. The ultimate aim of His creations is to build people.

As Artist-Disciples that is our work too. If we can really catch on to that principle in our hearts, then our lives will feel less like misery and more like ministry. We will want to range "through the whole world, anxious to bless the whole human race"[22] with our creations and with our love. This is the essence of Transformational Creation, which aspires to create like our Heavenly Father creates, at the highest level possible. In following lessons, we will explore Excellence and Secret

Ingredients, two other aspects of Transformational Creation that will enable us to be even more like our Father in Heaven in impacting those around us.

If achieved, Transformational Creation will eventually change the world—and us. Truly, as Arian said, "It is an amazing experience to be able to create with the Creator."

Questions and Action Items:

1. What experiences have you had with Transformational Creation? What makes these experiences "transformational"?

2. What is your "strategy"? List key components in your journal and consider how these could be adjusted to be even more effective.

3. How would you like to transform people who participate in your artistic endeavors?

Chapter Summary

- Although they might not always express it outwardly, everyone wants to be transformed. As Artist-Disciples, we are in a privileged position to lead individuals and societies toward positive transformation and joy.
- In opposition to Transformational Creation is Destructive Creation. Destructive Creation is a confuser and annoyer of the Lord's work and creates stumbling blocks to the positive changes the Lord desires us to affect through our creative work.

- Heavenly Father desires our creative works to be transformational, but more importantly, He desires us to be Transformational Creators. He desires us to not only do good, but to be good as well.
- Heavenly Father is the ultimate Transformational Creator and His work is all about creating transformation in people.
- Transformational Creation requires a lot out of us as Artist-Disciples, but the journey is worth it and the results are incredible. The results of Transformational Creation and Transformational Creators will be the Upstream.

---

[1] 2 Nephi 26:24.
[2] The Free Dictionary by Farlex, thefreedictionary.com/transformation, emphasis added.
[3] The Free Dictionary by Farlex, thefreedictionary.com/transform, emphasis added.
[4] The Free Dictionary by Farlex, thefreedictionary.com/creation.
[5] The Free Dictionary by Farlex, thefreedictionary.com/create.
[6] Tom Jackson, "A Great Show Doesn't Happen By Accident," blog.discmakers.com/2012/10/a-great-show-doesnt-happen-by-accident/.
[7] Cari Cole, *Step Up to the Spotlight: Kickstart Artist Development Program*, Cari Cole Voice & Music Co.
[8] Motoko Rich, "A Good Mystery: Why We Read," *New York Times*, November 25, 2007.
[9] 2 Nephi 2:25.
[10] "Principles of Member Missionary Work," missionaryleaders.org/node/30.
[11] Helaman 13:38.
[12] Alma 41:10.
[13] Moroni 7:45.
[14] Shanda Stiles, Visited The Bretts Show May 2012, tripadvisor.com/ShowUserReviews-g44160-d2332145-r132852114-The_Bretts-Branson_Missouri.html#REVIEWS.
[15] The Church of Jesus Christ of Latter-day Saints, *True to the Faith*, 132.
[16] Articles of Faith 1:13.
[17] James 3:10.
[18] Alma 39:11.
[19] Moses 1:39.
[20] 1 Nephi 17:36.
[21] Abraham 3:22-25.

[22] Joseph Smith, as quoted by Neil K. Newell, "Anxious to Bless the Whole Human Race," *Ensign,* April 1999.

Lesson 9:
Excellence

Artist-Disciple Insights

Kendra's Story: The Second Mile

"The second mile of hard work is what makes the difference between the exhilaration of achievement and the acceptance of mediocrity." (Wright, Randall. Achieving Your Life Mission. Springville, UT: Cedar Fort, Inc. 2009. Print.) I am an artist and I am a runner. Because of this, I enjoy the literal and figurative take on this quote equally. I have spent many of my last few miles of a run repeating this to myself, as I do when I am trying to push through frustration or long days and late nights.

I recently ran my first half marathon. 13.1 miles was something I had always wanted to achieve, but I was scared. That would mean 12 weeks of relentless training and would call for a great amount of commitment. I wasn't sure I had it in me. But I signed up, paid, and said a little prayer. I had no idea how much the experience would change my heart and open my eyes to the relationship between hard work and excellence. I trained 6 out of 7 days every week for 12 weeks. Come rain or scorching heat, I was outside kicking my heels. Sometimes it was at 4:30 a.m., other times it was at midnight. I ran that second mile, and the third, and the 8th, and so I went.

I reached a point in my training about 7 weeks into it where my knee started to give out and I almost couldn't complete any of my scheduled mileage. Instead of accepting that maybe I wasn't meant to be a runner and letting that barrier determine my defeat, I did some research, prayed a lot, and implemented different techniques and equipment into my daily regimen. Soon enough, my knee healed and the running technique I had developed was easier on my body and made the longer miles more manageable and enjoyable.

When I crossed that finish line and picked up my "13.1" medal, I felt that the world was mine, that I could do anything if I was willing to put in the hours and push through the fatigue. This lesson is *invaluable to me as a fitness fanatic, but even more so as an artist.*

The greatest difference as an artist happens within yourself and manifests through your art when you overcome your version of mediocrity. Trial and error is a part of the process and sometimes we will experience set-backs or failure, but that is only teaching us how to be more excellent. It's almost never going to be easy, nor is it going to be convenient. I don't know about you, but waking up at 4:30 in the morning to run 11 miles in the rain doesn't sound like something I would do for fun, or with a full schedule. But, when you love something and you have a passion and a purpose, you will push through the inevitable, unavoidable process that leads to excellence.

If we allow ourselves to shrink from the call to excellence as an Artist-Disciple, we are robbing the world of beauty and truth; ourselves of light, love, and understanding; and the Lord of perfecting and refining us. The first mile is hard and it does feel good after you have made it that far, but nothing compares to the exhilaration of achievement received after the second mile. That is where you will find those who have accepted the call and chosen to be chosen.

What makes the difference?

Ok, try this out:

List five to ten of your favorite artists, works of art, or experiences related to art.

Got it?

Now answer these questions:

What made those artists, works of art, or experiences related to art your "favorite?"

What are the ingredients that draw you to them?

Why do you remember them?

What do they do for you?

Are there any correlations between them and our discussion last lesson about Transformational Creation?

"I want to be better..."

Once in a TAD 101 course I was teaching, I took the class through a similar process. One class member's list looked something like this:

- Viewing beautiful tapestries of pictures of children's nursery rhymes in the lobby of a children's hospital.
- Seeing Sam Harris' performance of "Bridge Over Troubled Water."
- Seeing the London Ballet when I was fourteen years old.
- Reading the condensed version of "Les Miserables" aloud with my son.
- Reading a poem my sister had written.
- The first time I saw the ceiling in the Museum of Art in Vienna, Austria.
- Listening to the song "You Raise Me Up" for the first time.
- Hearing the recording of the King's Singers' "New Day," and then seeing them live and finding they were better live than recorded.
- Going to an Earth, Wind, and Fire concert—the most fun I'd ever had.
- Playing a Bach fugue "better than any student" my teacher had ever had.

Hopefully these responses spur more of your own. After pondering the questions I'd asked, this class member said,

> *All of those experiences hold a few things in common. [First is] the complete, undeniable* **excellence**— *they are so good at their craft. [In addition,] all of them displayed a* **passion** *and* **commitment** *to their art.*
>
> *Every single experience also made me feel* **closer to God** *because I so appreciate when I see someone who is trying to create something and they're doing it so well, because that's what our*

> *Heavenly Father and Jesus Christ have done. They are the ultimate Creators and when I see a human being do that same thing it literally thrills me and it changes me.*
>
> *And all of these experiences gave me…a visceral **feeling**. I had some kind of physical response to every single one. Either I would get chills, or it would make me cry. [Finally,] every single one of those things made me **want to be better**.*

Have you ever felt this way about an experience you had with an artist or work of art? I know I have. I'm sure we all have. Have you ever been transformed by experiencing the excellence of God's creation? As the ultimate Transformational Creators, Heavenly Father and Jesus Christ are our models for creating, and they always create in an undeniably excellent way.

Transformation Continues

In addition to what we learned in Lesson 8, there are five more ingredients to produce Transformational Creation. Today we're going to talk about one of them and we'll discuss the other four in our next lesson. Today's lesson is all about excellence, mastering our craft, working on our skills, and honing the *Personality Ethic*. By the time we're done, hopefully we'll be able to see clearly how excellence is really the foundation of Transformational Creation.

Meet the World and "Best" It

Let's revisit some bite-sized clips of previous quotations (and add a few new ones) to paint a picture of what we are destined to achieve:

> *Learn everything that the children of men know, and be prepared for the most refined society upon the face of the earth. Then improve on this until we are prepared and permitted to enter the*

society of the blessed—the holy angels, that dwell in the presence of God... – Brigham Young[1]

[The Prophet Joseph Smith] recommended that the Saints cultivate as high a state of perfection in their musical endeavors as possible. – Reid Nibley[2]

It was prophesied in a musical periodical in 1877 that the Church would have a music of its own and that it would be "universally cultivated as the highest branch of art." – Reid Nibley[3]

I'm convinced in my own mind that we have not really fulfilled our mission in life as individuals or as a Church 'til we have demonstrated as much advancement in other areas as we have in theology. – John Groberg[4]

If we strive for perfection—the best and greatest—and are never satisfied with mediocrity, we can excel. In the field of both composition and performance, why cannot someone write a greater oratorio than Handel's Messiah? *The best has not yet been composed nor produced. –* Spencer W. Kimball[5]

I hope we may produce men greater than this German composer, Wagner, but less eccentric, more spiritual. – Spencer W. Kimball[6]

Every accomplishment, every polished grace, every useful attainment in mathematics, music, and in all sciences and art belong to the Saints. – Brigham Young[7]

Go to, then, you who are gifted; cultivate your gift. Develop it in any of the arts and in every worthy example of them. If you have the ability and the desire, seek a career or employ your talent as an avocation or cultivate it as a hobby. But in all ways bless others with it. Set a standard of excellence... When we have done

> *it our activities will be a standard to the world.* – Boyd K. Packer[8]
>
> *The ideal, of course, is for one with a gift to train and develop it to the highest possibility, including a sense of spiritual propriety...He can meet the world and "best" it, and not be the loser...* – Boyd K. Packer[9]
>
> *Members of the Church should be peers or superiors to any others in natural ability, extended training, plus the Holy Spirit which should bring them light and truth. With hundreds of "men of God" and their associates so blessed, we have the base for an increasingly efficient and worthy corps of talent.* – Spencer W. Kimball[10]
>
> *A whole new generation of young, extremely talented music students has...added a new dimension to the musical potential...This may very well be the generation through which we can anticipate the fulfillment of the 1877 prophecy and by whom this people will be prepared to sing a new song unto the Lord.* – Reid Nibley[11]

For me, these quotations are at once inspiring, energizing and...overwhelming. It is clear that excellence is required to fulfill the gospel vision of the arts. But how can we achieve such a high level of expectation?

Well, I don't know exactly. I'm not perfect. Of all the lessons so far, I've struggled with this one the most. There are a lot of books dedicated to the subject of excellence and developing talents. I haven't written any of them. There is a lot of research out there as to what makes the truly high achievers realize their greatness. I'm not in those books. But, I can read and I do have a story of my own to share. So, let me share some of what I have learned from my reading and then take you on a journey through my process of achieving excellence in basketball.

Success, Talents, and Codes

In all of my research on excellence, three books kept rising to the top of the recommendation pile: Malcolm Gladwell's *Outliers: The Story of Success;* Daniel Coyle's *The Talent Code: Greatness Isn't Born. It's Grown. Here's How.;* and Geoff Colvin's *Talent is Overrated: What Really Separates World-Class Performers from Everybody Else.* Just the titles alone are insightful and exciting. I would HIGHLY recommend reading these books.

There are a lot of common components throughout all three of these titles and through all the existent research on this topic, but there doesn't seem to be an exact formula to achieving excellence. There is, however, a common idea through all of the research, and that is that *talent can be developed.* What appears to be "natural" or "born" can actually be developed. Your talent level is not "fixed" at birth.

We already learned about the interplay of agency and our premortal talents in previous lessons, so consider that in the equation as well. Assuming that you've been through the mission/offering decision process and that you've already selected in what domain you're going to focus on building skill, here are some very brief notes from these three great books. I will share just the tip of the iceberg so I don't spoil it for you when you get a chance to read these titles yourself:

- *10,000 Hour Rule.* From scientific research and case studies such as Bill Gates and The Beatles, Gladwell asserts that it takes approximately 10,000 hours to achieve mastery in a craft or domain.
- *Opportunities.* High-achievers and low-achievers are offered opportunities in life. Gladwell asserts that high-achievers actually take them and receive more opportunities as a consequence. This is a very thumbnail view of Gladwell's enlightening research on this topic but you get the idea.

- *Deep Practice and Deliberate Practice.* Both Colvin and Coyle share concepts of a different kind of practice—a more effective practice. It's not the hours you put in, necessarily. It's what you put into the hours. Both authors share groundbreaking research on getting the most out of your practice time.
- *Ignition.* We all know that excellence requires motivation, but Coyle uncovers the secret behind some of the world's highest achievers—a higher level of commitment he calls ignition. Ignition is born out of our deepest unconscious desires and is triggered by certain environmental or primal cues that ignite passion and become the catalyst for developing skill.

Humanity continues to progress above and beyond what we've done before. The above ingredients are some of the catalysts behind the improvement. As you seek excellence in your chosen field, it would be wise to seek out of the best books[12] and resources available the paths that other successful people have taken as well as the most current research on skill development, in order to optimize your path and ensure that you only build on the successes of the past and avoid repeating its time-wasting and poor habit-forming failures.

My Journey

When I was three years old, I decided I wanted to be a professional basketball player. From eighth grade on I became very serious about this goal and eventually received numerous offers from NCAA Division I and III schools, as well as NAIA schools. My feeling for basketball changed after I served my mission and I only ended up playing one year of college basketball at Southern Virginia University. As I described in the *Introduction*, I felt prompted to give up my spot on the team after that year and pursue art.

It was one of the hardest decisions I'd ever made because I had invested so much into basketball. But I've learned that the Lord was actually investing in me *through* basketball. He was teaching me portable principles in the process of perfection all along the way, and I'm now applying these principles in my new pursuits.

I am not going to pretend to know definitively the exact formula for achieving excellence. Instead I am going to tell a little bit of my story and hopefully uncover some advice, principles, and maxims for achieving excellence. These are things I've found to be true in my life as I've sought to overcome mediocrity.

1. Push Through Fear and Fatigue

President Eyring shared the following in the October 2011 Priesthood session:

> *Great priesthood trainers have shown me how to build [the strength to endure to the end]: it is to form a habit of pushing on through the fatigue and fear that might make you think of quitting. The Lord's great mentors have shown me that spiritual staying power comes from working past the point when others would have taken a rest.*[13]

Pistol Pete Maravich, who was one of my great basketball heroes growing up, said, "When you don't want to do it, that's when you do it ten times harder."[14] Steven Pressfield encouraged artists to be "warriors" and fight through "resistance" at all times[15] C.S. Lewis shared this quotation that hangs on the wall in my room:

> *There are always plenty of rivals to our work...If we let ourselves, we shall always be waiting for some distraction or other to end before we can really get down to our work. The only people who achieve much are those who want knowledge so badly that they*

seek it while the conditions are still unfavorable. Favorable conditions never come.[16]

Don't give up when the going gets tough. There are great rewards available to those who develop the habit of pushing through fear and fatigue when they feel like quitting.

2. *"Work hard and good things will happen"*

The quote above comes from another one of my great basketball heroes, Morgan Wootten. According to legendary coach John Wooden, Coach Wootten was the greatest basketball coach of all time. Coach Wootten routinely said things like, "It's the hard that makes it good," and he emphasized the ability of every player to maximize his or her potential if they just worked hard.

I love this quotation from Johann Sebastian Bach to a young student anxious about his ability to be a good pianist: "Just practice diligently, and it will go very well. You have five fingers on each hand just as healthy as mine."[17] I already shared the first part of the following quotation from psychologist William James in Lesson 6, but the latter half is my favorite as it relates to working hard:

> *...As we become permanent drunkards by so many separate drinks, so we become saints in the moral, and authorities and experts in the practical and scientific spheres by so many separate acts and hours of work. Let no youth have any anxiety about the upshot of his education, whatever the line of it may be. If he keeps faithfully busy every hour of the working day, he may safely leave the final result to itself. He can with perfect certainty count on waking up one fine morning, to find himself one of the competent ones of his generation, in whatever pursuit he may have singled out.*[18]

Chet Atkins shared his secrets to music success in these words: "It takes a lot of devotion and work, or maybe I should say play, because if you love it, that's what it amounts to. I haven't found any shortcuts, and I've been looking for a long time."[19]

Author Mary Heaton Vorse shared this piece of wisdom: "The art of writing is the art of applying the seat of the pants to the seat of the chair."[20]

To some, work is a four-letter word, but there's no way around it. The gospel of work is part of the gospel of Jesus Christ and it is part of achieving excellence in anything.

3. Extract Principles

Coach Wootten said, "The same things that make basketball work make life work."

This is true of excellence in any domain, skill, or field. The key is to develop the skill of extracting true principles out of the various practices and methods you encounter. Elder Richard G. Scott of the Quorum of the Twelve Apostles defines the idea of principles thusly:

> *Principles are concentrated truth, packaged for application to a wide variety of circumstances. A true principle makes decisions clear even under the most confusing and compelling circumstances. It is worth great effort to organize the truth we gather to simple statements of principle.*[21]

As I mentioned previously, I learned many principles of the process of perfection through basketball. These principles are portable and I'm now applying them as I strive to be an excellent musician and performing artist.

4. The Secret of the Fundamentals

Coach Wootten's Basketball Camp in Maryland was touted as the best teaching camp in the country. You can imagine that a seventh-grade boy who'd never been further east than Nauvoo would have high expectations for a camp with such a reputation. I arrived expecting to learn all the new moves, the secret plays, the playground tricks that would impress my friends when I got back home to Texas.

I was severely disappointed when Coach Wootten arose to address the camp for the first time, took a basketball in his hand, and announced, "Campers, this is a basketball." The next four days were dedicated to teaching such rudimentary skills as dribbling properly, shooting lay-ups correctly, and executing defensive slides. I was almost insulted. To add to the frustration, my camp team had not won a single game all week, and I was being out-skilled by all those gritty east coast players.

The night before camp ended I went to my dad, who was part of the coaching staff at the camp, and I sobbed, "Dad, I don't get it. I thought I'd come here and learn all the secrets, but all they're teaching us is how to shoot lay-ups. I already know all this stuff!" My dad patiently responded, "Son, don't you see it? You've been learning the secrets all along. *The fundamentals are the secrets.*"

For some reason, that truth came with great force into every feeling of my heart. It resonated with me as much as any truth has before or since. My dad was right. From that moment on I dedicated myself to mastering the fundamentals. I went back to camp for five years after that and received the Mr. Fundamental award—one of the highest awards given at the camp—four out of the five years. I was selected to demonstrate fundamentals in front of the whole camp year after year and eventually started running my own workshops and clinics. Not only that, because I mastered the fundamentals I was able to eventually learn the higher-level tricks and secrets.

In the gospel and in everything else, the fundamentals are the key to unlocking the mysteries. Mozart's quotation from Lesson 7 should have new meaning in this context:

> *The process with me is like a vivid dream....Ideas, clothed in the proper musical setting, stream down upon me. Of course, a composer must have mastered the technique of composition, form, theory, harmony, counterpoint, and instrumentation.*[22]

The Spirit cannot draw from an empty well, so master the fundamentals to give Him something to work with. You can then build the fancy stuff on top of your foundation of fundamentals.

5. Master Coaching: How to Choose a Mentor

Daniel Coyle discusses the principle of master coaching in *The Talent Code*. Although I would not say I was able to live up to all the ideals he sets forth in his book, I was still able to be trained by many great coaches. I have notes in my basketball binder from workshops I attended with NBA and college players and coaches like Hubie Brown, Billy Donovan, Joseph Forte, Danny Ferry, Steve Blake, Laron Profit, Steve Wojciechowski and many others. Add to that the numerous training videos and series I consumed and the great coaches I played for, and it is safe to say that I received great coaching.

Coaches and mentors are important. It is important, however, to be discerning in who you decide to learn from. Alma shared this counsel:

> *And also trust no one to be your teacher nor your minister, except he be a man of God, walking in his ways and keeping his commandments.*[23]

It might be impossible to find this type of person in your field of study, but the principle is true. Whoever you subscribe to as mentors and teachers, make sure you square all their teachings in Christ.

6. Success is Built on Inconvenience

One guest speaker at a basketball camp I attended shared an experience which has stuck with me. He was privileged to attend a coaching clinic at the University of North Carolina in Chapel Hill, NC, during the summer of 1992. It was the week after the Chicago Bulls had won their second world championship. On a lunch break, one of the UNC assistant coaches invited this man to take a ride with him. They drove into the parking lot of an old middle school and got out of the car. The temperature was sweltering— well over 100 degrees.

As they approached a large building on the school grounds, both the UNC assistant and this man could hear the faint sound of a ball bouncing on a hardwood floor and the squeaking of sneakers. They walked up to the open door of the un-air-conditioned gymnasium and gazed down the gym floor to see the silhouette of a tall, muscular, bald athlete spinning the basketball to himself, dripping with sweat as he nailed jump shot after jump shot. The UNC assistant called out, "Michael! I'd like you to meet somebody." Michael Jordan then walked over to the two of them, politely introduced himself to the man and went back to his workout. Seven days after winning the world championship, the best basketball player in the universe was in a tiny middle school gym in North Carolina, sweating it out—working on his game.

This impressed me so much that I resolved from the moment I heard it to work on my game no matter how inconvenient it was. I think I drove my family crazy, but I always found a way to get to a basketball court on road trips. Somehow I would get a complete 25-minute ball-handling workout in during our daily two-hour music performances. I'm not sure I would suggest the extremism I often demonstrated in my commitment to basketball (like sleeping with my basketball and taking it to school classes with me) but success is built on inconvenience. Are you in the business of looking good or are you in the business of getting better?

7. Who Are Your Companions?

I remember sitting next to a gentleman on a plane who, only two years prior, had been completely broke, at his lowest low. Now he sat next to me in designer jeans and lizard-skin boots, beaming with energy and enthusiasm as he shared his story. Of course I didn't know him before his apparent wealth, so I asked him what he had done to turn his life around. He said, "Programming, man. Programming."

I was confused. "What do you mean?" I asked. He pointed to his iPod. "If you want to be a millionaire, you gotta think like a millionaire. Millionaire thoughts lead to millionaire actions. Millionaire actions lead to millionaire results." He explained further. "Every day I put on my headphones and listen to positive, uplifting stuff. It programs me to be successful. This iPod is the best investment I've ever made."

Now I don't believe he meant that the iPod was the reason his life turned around, but isn't it interesting that what you put into your brain is what comes out of your brain? If you put bad fuel in your car it will stop running. Studies at the University of Southern California showed that if you lived in a metropolitan area, drove 12,000 miles per year, and listened to books and audio recordings as you drove, in three years you could acquire the equivalent of two years of college education.[24]

Author Joshua Harris wrote the following about music but it applies to anything we feed our mind with:

> *Good music can move our hearts to love God; ungodly music can entice us to love sin. No person is immune to the influence of music with sinful content. The musicians we listen to become our companions, and God says the companion of fools will suffer harm (Prov. 13:20). Who are your companions? What's in your CD or MP3 player?*[25]

I don't know who your companions are, but I can tell you this—you're better off hanging out with President Monson than Lady Gaga. As you seek to learn all that the children of men know and try to overcome the world by knowledge, it will be important to remember this advice from President Packer: "There is a big difference between *studying* something and studying *about* something."[26] Don't sacrifice your standards to learn what the world has to offer.

In any case, this whole idea of programming seems to be part of the process of excellence. All the greats I've studied also studied the greats. To be a successful person, do what successful people do. As we learn what the giants before us have known, we can then build on their shoulders. Your thoughts are where excellence begins, so take control of your programming.

8. Dream Big Dreams, Make a Plan, Make it Happen

This simple formula inspired me as an eighth-grader to really get serious about my dream of becoming a professional basketball player. I had the dream, but I did not have the plan and, consequently, I was not making it happen in the most efficient way. I learned the importance of making a plan and then working your plan and that's exactly what I did. Along the way I learned some other valuable lessons.

Daily discipline. It is better to practice 30 minutes per day than 30 hours every other week. Consistency is king in achieving excellence. You may be familiar with this quotation from Jim Rohn. "We must all suffer from one of two pains: the pain of discipline or the pain of regret. The difference is discipline weighs ounces while regret weighs tons."[27]

Legendary football coach Paul Bryant is quoted as saying, "It's not the will to win, but the will to prepare to win that makes the difference."[28] We've already discussed stepping up your daily habits and practices in both the *Personality Ethic* and the *Character Ethic*. It is in the daily where I see most Artist-Disciples falling flat in their pursuit of excellence.

Keep records. My dad encouraged me to keep a checklist of all my drills and routines daily. I had charts and spreadsheets and I was religious about keeping on top of them. It was motivating to see my progress and I feel like I progressed much more rapidly because I kept myself accountable to my daily routine in this way.

Feedback and evaluation. Built into my weekly routine was an end-of-week progress assessment. I would get my dad or a coach to give me some evaluation on what I needed to improve on. I would also time myself and push myself to best my past week's record in each drill. In this way I gained valuable feedback as to what I needed to improve on. This isn't the only way to do it, but the principle of receiving feedback and evaluation is very important to speed your progress.

Achievable Idealism

In all our discussion of the elements it takes to achieve excellence, we need to make sure that what we set out to do is what we truly want and what will bring us the most happiness.

How do we know which dreams to invest our time in? I'd like to share my personal view on this. The following process has helped me as I've tried to distinguish between mortal pipe dreams and dreams that I should actually spend my time, energy and resources pursuing. I call it the Achievable Idealism Model.

Step 1: Idealism. I'm a dreamer. I think most Artist-Disciples are. When a spark or an idea is seeded in my mind, I get excited. I think of all the grand possibilities. I play out all the successful scenarios and ask, "Why not?" My mind immediately shoots for the stars. This is more than an infatuation phase; it is an important part of the process. We need to allow ourselves to think about our big and important goals. We need to allow ourselves to feel energized by them. We must allow this Idealism Phase to expand our vision and really *feel* it, but if our dream is ever going to do anything, we must take it through the next step.

Step 2: Realism. Sometimes when people say they are realists, they tend to be more like pessimists. There is no need to be pessimistic about your dream, but if you ever want your dream to become a reality, you have to go through a reality phase. During this step I take my dreams or ideas through two tests.

- *The Three Rings Test.* Does this dream or idea align with the Three Rings and help me to fulfill my purposes within each?
- *The Luke 14:28 Test.* "For which of you, intending to build a tower, sitteth not down first, and counteth the cost, whether he have sufficient to finish it?"[29] This test is crucial. Before you start, you have to assess if you have what it takes to *finish* building your dream.

If your dream does not pass both tests, then you have to question if it is something you should pursue. Throughout all of this, think in solutions, not problems; in challenges, not obstacles. Be positive and realistic and strive for creative solutions with faith.

Step 3: Achievable Idealism. If the dream passes Step 2, then you have an executable dream or idea. Not only does it feel good, it *is* good and there is a high probability that it can actually happen.

Of course this is not a hard and fast rule. Many dreams have been accomplished that were never considered achievable (just read the scriptures). But by and large, the Lord expects us to use wisdom in selecting how to use our time on this earth. For me it's part of studying it out in my mind[30] and bringing my stones before the Lord so He can touch them with His finger.[31]

Achievable Idealism returns to you much of the infatuation and energy of Step 1 with the added excitement that your dream won't always just be a dream.

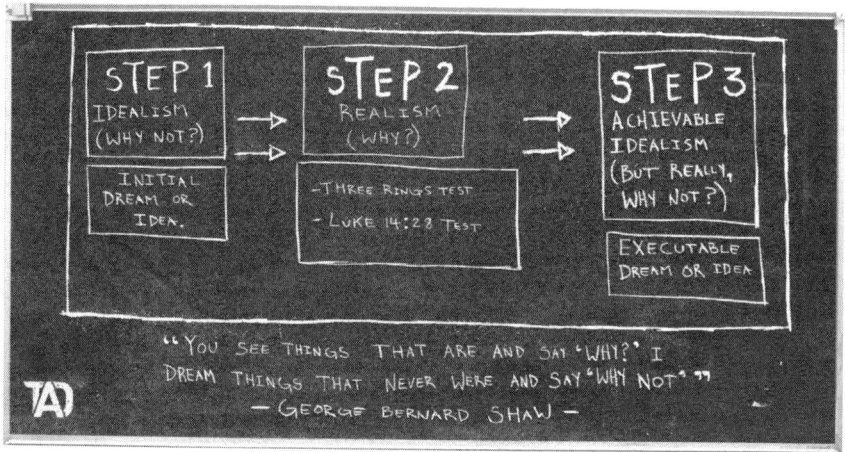

Learn For Yourself

Hopefully these stories and principles have been helpful to you. There are many more I could share, but for now I would just like to invite you to be a diligent and hungry student of excellence. The process of excellence isn't something you can learn from a book. You have to learn it for yourself. I am learning new things every day that help me to become more and more excellent and successful as an artist.

If you really want to create transformationally, then you've got to become serious about mastering your craft. But, don't procrastinate creating just because you're not perfect yet. Remember, excellence does not necessarily require mastery. You can create excellent things along your road to mastery. If you wait for perfection, then you'll find the truth in this anonymous proverb, "It's always too early, until it's too late."

Three Phases: Imitation, Innovation, Imagination

Once you have made a plan and begun to apply the principles of excellence, realize that there is an artist-development arc you will go through as you seek to create something truly transformational. Each of these three phases is an essential part of learning to create something of truly impactful excellence as an Artist-Disciple.

The first is *Imitation*. When you first start out as an Artist-Disciple, you imitate. Think about it. You copy vocal licks, jokes, facial expressions, you even dress up like your favorite stars. This is okay in the artistic process because style is more caught than taught. But the world won't put up with you for too long if you're merely a "hack" or a copycat. It is like an apartment complex. All of the apartments have the same floor plan. They all look the same. This is the imitation phase.

The next phase is *Innovation*. You take component parts and put them together in unique ways, perhaps in ways that have never been seen before. You've moved past imitation. When you move into an apartment and bring all of your decorations, furniture and possessions with you, the apartment takes on a new flavor. It becomes yours. This is innovation.

The third phase is *Imagination*. This is where you are creating things that have never been created before. It is like remodeling—totally coming up with a new floor plan or moving to a different apartment concept altogether. This is the realm where the trendsetters and leaders live. It's the kind of creation that can form the Upstream.

Standard of Excellence

As we've discussed excellence today, I believe that the ultimate destiny of Artist-Disciples is, like Brigham Young said, to learn from the world and then "improve on" it. As we are faithful, disciplined and diligent, the Lord will bless us with revelation, the right people coming into our lives, and increased capacity to develop this kind of creativity. Eventually people will be writing about how our creation transformed them. Our creation will become a standard of excellence for the world.

Questions and Action Items:

1. If you haven't already, go through the entire exercise described at the beginning of this chapter. List 5-10 of your favorite works of art and artistic experiences, and then go through and take notes. What makes these your favorites? How can you incorporate some of these elements into your own life?

2. What are 2-3 areas of your life in which you can "step up your daily"? Make a list of places to improve, then pick one and apply it in your life. Watch and see how your skills increase through daily effort in your craft.

3. Who are the "excellent" ones in your craft? How can you make them your companions?

Chapter Summary

- Excellence is a common ingredient in works of Transformational Creation.
- As Artist-Disciples, we are expected to strive for excellence. We can meet the world and "best" it.
- There is a lot of research on talent development, being successful and achieving excellence. It is worth your time and effort to seek these principles out and apply them.
- Excellence is a complex objective with many components. Seek the Lord's help to know the most important components for your pursuit of excellence.
- Excellence, almost without exception, involves the three phases of Imitation, Innovation and Imagination. Don't give up and you will eventually arrive at imagination and really help form the Upstream.

---

[1] Brigham Young, as quoted by Spencer W. Kimball, "Education for Eternity," BYU Annual Faculty Conference, September 12, 1967.
[2] Reid Nibley, "Thoughts on Music in the Church," 1972.
[3] Nibley, "Thoughts on Music in the Church," 1972.
[4] John Groberg, "What is Your Mission?" BYU Devotional, May 01, 1979.
[5] Spencer W. Kimball, "The Gospel Vision of the Arts," *Ensign,* July 1977.
[6] Kimball, "The Gospel Vision of the Arts," *Ensign,* July 1977.
[7] Brigham Young, as quoted by Spencer W. Kimball, "The Gospel Vision of the Arts," *Ensign,* July 1977.
[8] Boyd K. Packer, "The Arts and the Spirit of the Lord," BYU Fireside, February 01, 1976.
[9] Packer, "The Arts and the Spirit of the Lord," BYU Fireside, February 01, 1976.
[10] Kimball, "The Gospel Vision of the Arts," *Ensign,* July 1977.
[11] Nibley, "Thoughts on Music in the Church," 1972.
[12] Doctrine and Covenants 88:118.
[13] Henry B. Eyring, "Preparation in the Priesthood: 'I Need Your Help'" *Ensign,* November 2011.
[14] Pete Maravich, *Pistol Pete's Homework Basketball,* LA Production Group, Inc.
[15] Stephen Pressfield, *The War of Art: Break Through the Blocks and Win Your Inner Creative Battles.*

[16] C.S. Lewis, "Learning in War-Time," 10.
[17] Johann Sebastian Bach, http://www.christians.com/inspirational/jsbach_for_the_glory_of_god.
[18] William James, as quoted by Maria Popova, "William James on Habit," brainpickings.org/index.php/2012/09/25/william-james-on-habit/.
[19] Chet Atkins, newagepianism.com/2010/12/music-quotes/.
[20] Mary Heaton Vorse, *Beating the Odds: Getting Published in the Field of Literacy*, 34.
[21] Richard G. Scott, "Acquiring Spiritual Knowledge," *Ensign,* November 1993.
[22] Wolfgang Amadeus Mozart, walterrobinsmusic.com/vivid-dream-part-2.html.
[23] Mosiah 23:14.
[24] Zig Ziglar, *How to Be a Winner,* Simon & Schuster Audio.
[25] Joshua Harris, *Sex Is Not the Problem (Lust Is): Sexual Purity in a Lust-Saturated World,* 69.
[26] Boyd K. Packer, *The Essence of Education, Let Not Your Heart Be Troubled,* 22-30.
[27] Jim Rohn, goodreads.com/quotes/209560-we-must-all-suffer-from-one-of-two-pains-the.
[28] Paul Bryant, thechangeblog.com/success-principles/.
[29] Luke 14:28.
[30] Doctrine and Covenants 9:7-9.
[31] Ether 3:4.

Lesson 10:
The Secret Ingredients

Artist-Disciple Insights

Jesse-Elyce's Story: Profane Poet

I am currently enrolled in an art and activism class that frequently sponsors community art events. The beautiful fellowship of students cultivated by these events is as eclectic as it is unified. Participants knowledgeable in nearly every discipline, common and unique, meet and commune, expressing their lifeblood with one another.

One particular fellow stood out to me for more reasons than one. It was apparent he was quite talented, well dressed, accomplished and had many friends. But, unfortunately he seemed to know this a little too well himself. His haughty attitude cast a shadow around his visage as he approached the microphone to share one of his poems. With a smirk, he began what turned out to be one of the most irreverent, profaning performances I'd seen. His technique and talent with words and symbolism were undeniable, and by the world's standards, he was an artist. But I knew differently.

I know that true artists are not only just inspired, but they inspire others. They do not simply pander to the basest of human appetites, but strive to lift the natural man out of earshot and cast it away. Through the God-given talents given him, this man could have encouraged good in those around him but instead his creations were degradational and not transformational in nature. His words would last only till the next shock or snare diverted attention, and then die. This poor man's ministry was to sow misery of soul, and he would gain no respect from it.

Coming from Hollywood

I once had a phone conversation with a fairly well-known and eccentric Hollywood producer. He was interested in somehow exploiting the brand of entertainment my family was offering. I explained to him a little of our vision to produce good, clean, wholesome and excellently-done family entertainment.

He stopped me in the middle of my explanation and said, "You have no idea how big the market is for what you're doing. People are tired of having this filth crammed down their throat. My grandson sits there in front of the TV all day and watches all this garbage. He learns about drugs and sex and violence and profanity. I'm tired of it too. If anybody is going to teach my grandson how to swear, it's going to be me, not some guy on a TV screen!"[1]

Does that happen frequently?

How often do people want something different than what the world has to offer, but hesitate to take the small or large steps it takes to get there?

I thought the whole conversation was interesting—interesting that there is a huge market for the good and the wholesome, but also interesting that this grandfather, the movie producer, was sitting, not standing, for righteousness as he let his grandson get educated by Babylon.

President Hinckley's Perspective

> *One evening I picked up the morning paper, which I had not previously read, and thumbed through its pages. My eyes stopped on the theater ads, so many of them an open appeal to witness that which is debauching, that which leads to violence and illicit sex.*
>
> *I turned to my mail and found a small magazine which lists the television fare for the coming week and saw titles of shows aimed in the same direction. A news magazine lay on my desk. This particular issue was devoted to the rising crime rate. Articles in the magazine spoke of additional billions for increased police forces and larger prisons.*
>
> *The flood of pornographic filth, the inordinate emphasis on sex and violence are not peculiar to North America. The situation is as bad in Europe and in many other areas. The whole dismal picture indicates a weakening rot seeping into the very fiber of society.*
>
> *Legal restraints against deviant moral behavior are eroding under legislative enactments and court opinions. This is done in the name of freedom of speech, freedom of the press, freedom of choice in so-called personal matters. But the bitter fruit of these so-called freedoms has been enslavement to debauching habits and behavior that leads only to destruction. A prophet, speaking long ago, aptly described the process when he said, "And thus the devil cheateth their souls, and leadeth them away carefully down to hell (2 Nephi 28:21)."*[2]

Those words were from a previous prophet and president of the Church. Is he right? As Artist-Disciples, can we truly stem the tide of evil? Do we have what it takes to compete against the morally eroding filth and garbage in the arts and entertainment world? Can we truly create light-filled work that will make a difference?

From this despondent tone Gordon B. Hinckley then turned to an attitude of hope and optimism as he described his vision for what could be:

> *On the other hand, I am satisfied that there are millions upon millions of good people in this and in other lands. For the most part, husbands are faithful to wives, and wives to husbands. Their children are being reared in sobriety, industry, and faith in God.*
>
> *Given the strength of these, I am one who believes that the situation is far from hopeless. I am satisfied that there is no need to stand still and let the filth and violence overwhelm us or to run in despair.* **The tide, high and menacing as it is, can be turned back** *if enough of the kind I have mentioned will add their strength to the strength of the few who are now effectively working. I believe the challenge to oppose this evil is one from which members of The Church of Jesus Christ of Latter-day Saints, as citizens, cannot shrink.*[3]

I believe he is right! It is not too late. We have not yet reached that dreaded point described by Mosiah when the "voice of the people doth choose iniquity."[4] We may, however, be rapidly approaching this state if we don't take swift action. I have no reservations in joining with President Hinckley and saying that there are "millions upon millions of good people" in the world whom we can influence if we will step up and not shrink from the challenge. The point remains: a lot of people want something different.

Time to Awaken Transformation

As an Artist-Disciple, do you feel a sense of urgency about what is happening in the world and your role in opposing wickedness? Do you understand the need to stand, not sit, for righteousness? In choosing to do so, I believe we'll experience more, not less, of the victories that Elder Neal A. Maxwell described in this statement:

> *Before the ultimate victory of the forces of righteousness, some skirmishes will be lost... There will also be times, happily, when a minor defeat seems probable, that others will step forward, having been rallied to righteousness by what we do. We will know the joy, on occasion, of having awakened a slumbering majority of the decent people of all races and creeds—a majority which was, till then, unconscious of itself.*[5]

We are on the winning team. There is a "slumbering majority" out there just waiting to be "rallied to righteousness" by what we do.

Can we rise to this challenge? Of course we can, and we most certainly will!

Where do we start?

President Hinckley suggested four "points of beginning" in our efforts to oppose the tide of evil:

1. Begin with yourself;
2. A better tomorrow begins with the training of a better generation;
3. The building of public sentiment begins with a few earnest voices;
4. Strength to do battle begins with enlisting the strength of God.[6]

Each one of these steps can be practiced in all of the work we do in our Three Rings and as creators, and we can begin today. Grounded in these "points of beginning," we can then move swiftly into the Upstream with four more secret ingredients that will turn back the tide. Contrasted to the world's ingredients, the Lord's secret ingredients will initiate Transformational Creation, and we will become Transformational Creators in the process.

The World's Ingredients

At the beginning of this chapter, TAD graduate Jesse-Elyce shared her experience with a poet who was skilled but not uplifting. Did you notice what was highlighted by this man's performance? First, his work was degrading and irreverent, and was not about to transform anyone into anything good. But second, he had talent and technique. Therefore, he had an audience that would listen to him. Since you woke up this morning, how many times have you seen examples just like this?

In the arena of art and entertainment, there are five common ingredients I see in almost everything that is produced by the Mainstream:

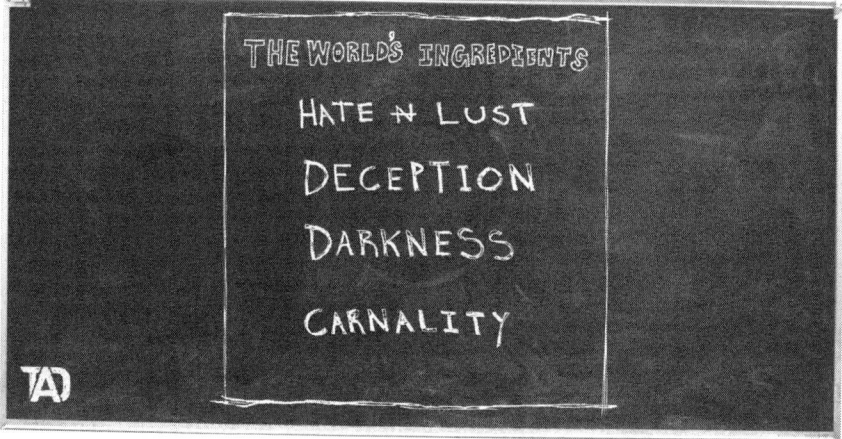

Most art or creative work in the Mainstream shares some or all of these ingredients, and certainly the morally deteriorating creations do. These are the tools that Satan has been using in the arts and entertainment for centuries, and they are powerful. They are powerful because they appeal to the natural man, the path of least resistance, the carnal, the sensual, the devilish in all of us. They are powerful because they lead to addictions (immediate gratification that then needs to be satisfied again and again,) a false sense of power, a temporary "high," an escape, rationalized behavior, and materialism. They are powerful because they lead people to a false sense of that joy we are all seeking. It won't last, but they hope it will so they return to it time after time.

Recipe for Decay

Playwright Noel Coward said, "[It's] Extraordinary how potent cheap music is."[7] In this sense I don't think Mr. Coward meant cheap as in inexpensive. No, I believe he meant the cheap laugh, the cheap thrill, the cheap carnal reaction. Why do you think pornography is such a pandemic? Actually, inexpensive would not be the word at all because, in fact, the world's ingredients are often packaged in such excellence, appeal, polish, professionality and financial resources that they become almost impossible to ignore. Think about all the money and resources and talent in the Mainstream today!

When you combine this excellence with the world's ingredients, you have a "potent" recipe that has led to much of the moral and spiritual decay in society, preventing the opportunity for the gospel vision we have been discussing.

The Lord's Ingredients

When it comes to the transformational for good in arts and entertainment, there are four secret ingredients that I see in almost all of it. These are the Lord's ingredients that Satan seeks to counter. They are the opposition (2 Nep. 2:11) to Satan's offerings.[8] And here's the good news—they are powerful! More powerful, in fact, than the world's ingredients. They are:

In all of my "favorite" artists, art, or experiences related to art, some or all of these ingredients have been present. Transformational Creation calls for these ingredients in its recipe. Love overpowers hate and lust. Truth overcomes deception. Light chases away darkness. The Spirit has the power to change carnal to spiritual. This is the nature of the universe. These things naturally have more power than their worldly counterparts.

As Artist-Disciples it is our opportunity to use these tools to bring true happiness to people, to help them find what they're really looking for, which is light, joy, and peace.

We have our work cut out for us because the world's ingredients are so pervasive that they have cast a thick secular smog over the entire world. These mists of darkness have clouded people's minds as to what true joy really is and how to find it, but we can counter it by incorporating the Lord's tools into all of our creations.

Too good to be true?

But wait, isn't something missing? This all sounds too good to be true. It is. Because, sadly, the secret ingredients don't seem to get much traction unless you meet the world on its own terms and add in that important fifth ingredient:

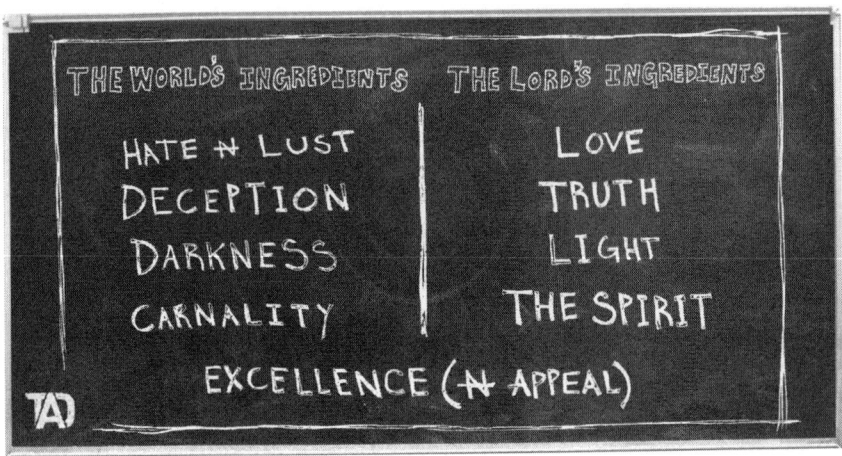

Excellence + The Secret Ingredients = Transformational Creation

Excellence is the common denominator between the Lord's way and the adversary's way. It is excellence that will get the world to listen or pay attention; the Lord's ingredients will then transform them. Without excellence and appeal, it seems that the Lord's ingredients are destined to be in the Downstream, forever perceived as hokey, cheesy, not professional, low-quality, "not cool."

Does it really take excellence?

You might say that it doesn't take excellence for people to feel the Spirit through your performance. I would totally agree. I've been to many a sacrament meeting where the humble offering of one of the Lord's weak and simple servants helped me feel the Spirit more than an "excellent" performance from one of the trained musicians in the congregation.

Please understand that I'm not saying that you have to be excellent to produce things that have the Lord's ingredients in them—things that can transform people. We've already discussed that in previous lessons. But what I am saying is that, in the Mainstream, a lack of excellence is distracting. It makes it so that the Lord's ingredients are hardly ever able to get through and move people.

When you combine the professionalism, appeal, polish and excellence of the world (and better) with the Lord's ingredients, the effect can be powerful. The result is the Upstream. I see many examples in the Church of Artist-Disciples already "effectively working" in this way. We are starting to stem the tide of evil. If we continue and don't get caught in the current of the Mainstream, we will eventually form the new Upstream.

But what about Lady Gaga?

One question you might have in all of this discussion on excellence and the Lord's ingredients is, "What about artists like Lady Gaga, Madonna, or the other popular artists I see on *America's Got Talent,* who do not appear to be excellent but still get through to the Mainstream?"

Note what American jazz guitarist Tal Farlow had to say about this:

> *For something to gain so much popularity and appeal for so many people, it has to be either musically valid [EXCELLENT] or so*

> *commercial that you can't ignore it [APPEALING], especially if your living depends on it. Jazz has never really reached that kind of popularity and I don't think it ever will, because you're actually playing for musicians and musicians are not a good crowd to play for. If you are going to try and make some money, you've got to appeal to a wider area than that.*[9]

This is an interesting quotation and there is a lot to learn from it. For our purposes, Tal has just illuminated the principle that some things that gain popularity won't be excellent. They will be so commercial that the public can't ignore them—hence, the sordid, the sensational, the shocking, and the controversial things that become popular in the Mainstream. In these types of things, Artist-Disciples just let the chips fall where they may, as it were. Don't worry about trying to compete in that world. But Artist-Disciples should be very concerned with producing commercial-quality material—material that is excellent enough to compete on a commercial level.

But that sounds hard

Top-level artistry can be challenging, especially at the accelerating rate of technological change. But the technological landscape of the world right now is tailor-made to give us access to all of the resources we need to produce excellent content.

The Internet has lifted us to a golden age of information that has equalized the playing field for excellence in many respects. We have software, hardware, tutorials and other informational resources at our fingertips that can put us on a plane with even the best in our chosen fields. Even on a low budget, with some ingenuity, we can create commercial-level material in many of the arts. I mention this to give hope to those of us who don't have access to Hollywood studios, the Louvre, or a Broadway stage. We can still move more and more toward the ideal if we're hungry enough. The Artist-Disciple stage is constantly expanding, and there is no reason we cannot participate in it.

What is your niche?

Another benefit that the Internet brings is the ability to reach niche markets. People who are likely to like you can actually find you and you can actually find people who are likely to like you. It does take effort. The Internet is not a silver bullet, but its possibilities are exciting, and over time we will reach and surpass the world and become the leaders and trend-setters in pioneering excellence. To do this requires that we seek knowledge and revelation, which leads to power.

I think this is a very interesting quotation from the Prophet Joseph Smith:

> *A man is saved no faster than he gets knowledge, for if he does not get knowledge, he will be brought into captivity by some evil power in the other world, as evil spirits will have more knowledge, and consequently more power than many men who are on the earth. Hence it needs revelation to assist us, and give us knowledge of the things of God.*[10]

I think this holds true for evil spirits and for those in the Mainstream. As long as they have more knowledge than we have, they will have more power than we have. But it is not intended that Satan and his angels should outwit, outsmart, or out-skill us. We can and will gain knowledge of the world and of the things of God and gain the power we need to create excellent things.

But that sounds boring

Truman G. Madsen, author and professor of religion and philosophy at Brigham Young University, said, "Don't take yourself so seriously that when you walk down the street people look at you and say, 'Three cheers for sin!'"[11]

If you think it sounds boring to produce Transformational Creation, then you are probably just misinformed about the incredible dynamic range of emotion and feeling and joy to be experienced in the gospel of Jesus Christ. Consider these quotations:

> *...the nearer man approaches perfection, the clearer are his views, and the greater his enjoyments, till he has overcome the evils of his life and lost every desire for sin...* – Joseph Smith[12]

> *The gift of the Holy Spirit adapts itself to all these organs and attributes. It quickens all the intellectual faculties, increases, enlarges, expands, and purifies all the natural passions and affections, and adapts them by the gift of wisdom, to their lawful use. It inspires, develops, cultivates, and matures all the fine-tone sympathies, joys, tastes, kindred feelings, and affections of our nature. It inspires virtue, kindness, goodness, tenderness, gentleness, and charity. It develops beauty of person, form and features. It tends to health, vigor, animation, and social feeling. It develops and invigorates all the faculties of the physical and intellectual man. It strengthens, invigorates, and gives tone to the nerves. In short, it is, as it were, marrow to the bone, joy to the heart, light to the eyes, music to the ears, and life to the whole being.*

> *In the presence of such persons, one feels to enjoy the light of their countenances, as the genial rays of a sunbeam. Their very atmosphere diffuses a thrill, a warm glow of pure gladness and sympathy, to the heart and nerves of others who have kindred feelings, or sympathy of spirit.* – Parley P. Pratt[13]

Taking ourselves too seriously misses the point. Producing Transformational Creation does not mean that all of our work has to be "pious and holy," which, to many of us, means the same thing as "boring."

As members of the Church of Jesus Christ of Latter-day Saints, our temples are masterpieces of beauty and excellence, and they are anything but boring. With the Lord's ingredients, our creation can be a fruits-of-the-Spirit buffet—a wide-ranging gamut of love, joy, peace, goodness, gentleness, hope, energy, excitement, vigor, animation, social feeling and connection.

The Lord's ingredients expand our creative color wheel; the world's ingredients actually contract it—everything starts looking and tasting the same. Perhaps the greatest miracle of seeking to produce Transformational Creation is that leading others to the joy and excitement of the gospel will require us to find it, feel it and internalize it ourselves. The point is not to dilute the Lord's way; the purpose is to show just how amazing the Lord's way really is.

Power and Popularity

Too many well-meaning artists in and out of the Church neutralize the Lord's power by not using His ingredients. This makes no sense. Why compete with Satan using His weapons, weaker weapons, or no weapons at all? Why not get on his playing field with more powerful tools?

All four of the Lord's secret ingredients are more powerful than their counterparts, but they may not necessarily be more popular at first. I believe they must be wrapped in excellence to become popular and appealing. These secret ingredients fall on both sides of Character Ethic and Personality Ethic. They represent what we can and should become, as well as what we can use as tools in our creation. The effective combination of these ingredients with excellence, plus the correct Character and Personality Ethic balance, will produce Transformational Creation.

I hope that we will use these four ingredients and President Hinckley's four points of beginning as we seek to infuse our creation, and our personal becoming, with love, light, truth, and the Spirit. Let's stem the tide of evil. Let's wake up those slumbering millions upon millions. Let's go Upstream.

Questions and Action Items

1. How do you recognize the Lord's "secret ingredients" in art and media today? List examples of art that exemplifies each of these secret ingredients.

2. How often do you see the world's ingredients in art on a daily basis? List some examples of this as well.

3. Looking at your examples from each of these areas, compare them. Why are excellence and appeal so important?

4. Why are the Lord's ingredients more powerful? How can you use them more in your life?

Chapter Summary

- Although the world is becoming increasingly more degenerate, we can rest assured that we are on the winning team. The tide of evil can be turned if the millions and millions of good people throughout the

world become unified. As an Artist-Disciple, you have an important role to play in this unification process.
- When it comes to works of art, the world's ingredients are hate, deception, darkness and carnality
- When it comes to the Lord's way of creating art, the secret ingredients are love, truth, light, and the Spirit. The Lord's ingredients are more powerful than their worldly counterparts.
- Excellence is the common denominator between the world's ingredients and the Lord's ingredients
- Excellence combined with the secret ingredients will infuse your creative works with the power to cut through the noise and become popular and appealing.

---

[1] Personal interview with the author.
[2] Gordon B. Hinckley, "In Opposition to Evil," *Ensign,* September 2004.
[3] Hinckley, "In Opposition to Evil," *Ensign,* September 2004.
[4] Mosiah 29:27.
[5] Neal A. Maxwell, "Meeting the Challenges of Today," BYU Devotional, October 10, 1978.
[6] Hinckley, "In Opposition to Evil," *Ensign,* September 2004.
[7] Noel Coward, brainyquote.com/quotes/quotes/n/noelcoward156778.html.
[8] 2 Nephi 2:11.
[9] Tal Farlow, 12tonemusic.com/MrPick/quotes.shtml.
[10] Joseph Smith, as quoted by Randal Wright, *Achieving Your Life Mission,* 92.
[11] Truman G. Madsen, "The Highest in Us," BYU Devotional, March 3, 1974.
[12] Joseph Smith, as quoted by Neal A. Maxwell, *Not My Will, But Thine,* 81.
[13] Parley P. Pratt, *Key to the Science of Theology,* 101.

Section IV: Influence

Lesson 11:
Influence

Artist-Disciple Insights

Dallin's Story: Fame and Leadership

I have been on stage since I was two. Throughout my life I have experienced public recognition of my talent and accomplishment from young and old. As I've reflected on what goes on inside my mind during these experiences, it seems to me that being famous is just like any other job...in a way.

That way is how you feel about it.

You see, just like any other job in life, it can become ordinary, slow, hum-drum and even bothersome if you let it. You really have to care if you want to succeed, because people can tell if you care about them or not.

To illustrate this point, I want to share the experience I had performing for two different youth groups.

On one hand, youth group #1 came to a performance that didn't turn out so well. I wasn't connected to the audience because something happened earlier that day that I let affect my emotional state. My emotional distance affected my performance. People want artists to be real and present with them, and I wasn't.

On the other hand, youth group #2 was there on a day that had gone by as though the sun was smiling and there was a nice breeze keeping everything smooth and flowing. I was attentive and happy to be there.

Group #1 was a wonderful group, but I wasn't focused on them and they could tell my mind was elsewhere. I went to talk to them after the performance and they didn't want to stay and talk with me. I don't know if they could tell I didn't give them 100%, but something was off.

Compare that to group #2. Through the entire performance, I connected with them. They then wanted to synergize with me. They saw me giving 100% and in return, they wanted to give their 100% back.

This all brings me to the conclusion that being famous isn't about jewels, cars or the latest fashion. Fame is leadership. People who focus on those material things are missing out because the most important things in this life are the relationships each individual has in their circle of influence. Being famous is about being a leader and that requires you to like the title and responsibilities that come with it.

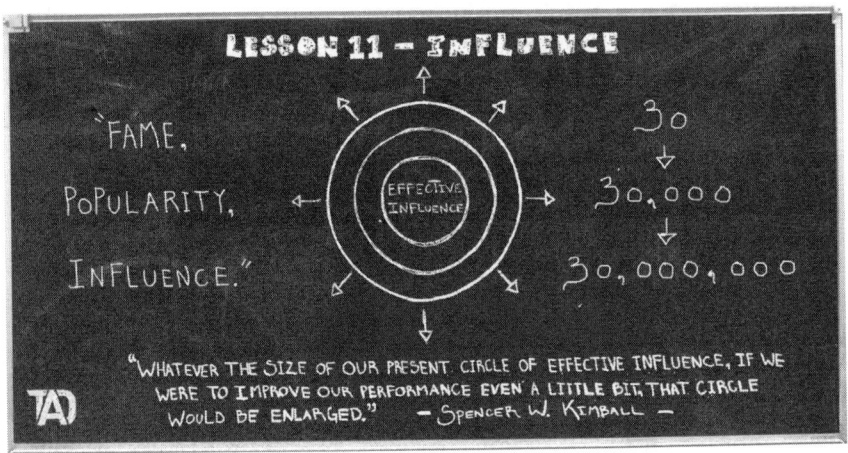

Time to Be Noticed

As an Artist-Disciple, what is your perspective on fame?

Side 1: I don't want to be famous. I'm not interested in fame.

I remember a conversation I once had with an artist who had been in the entertainment business for a long time. When he was younger he had experienced some relatively big success which, for a brief time, led to a pretty serious dose of fame. At the time I talked to him he was also very successful, supporting his family through music, composing, performing, and doing what he loved to do but on a much less public level. He told me, "I've experienced my share of fame. I don't want to be famous. I'm not interested in fame. I just want to have my family and continue doing what I'm doing. I'll be happy with that."

Side 2: You have to be famous. Fame allows you to have influence.

On the flip side of the debate is another conversation I had with one of my music mentors in Nashville, TN. As I discussed my music goals with her I said, "For me, it's not about fame, it's about influence. I'm not trying to be famous…" She stopped me mid-sentence: "No, but you have to be famous. You see, fame allows you to have influence. Fame is how you get to people."

Which side of the camp do you find yourself on?

Get Comfortable

Now that we've discussed the idea of Transformational Creation and wrapped up our examination of steps to forming the Upstream, it's time to talk about something that we all deal with as Artist-Disciples. Creative and artistic work is typically made to be noticed, to be heard, to be seen, to be read, to be experienced, to make a statement, to make a difference, to teach, to spark, to influence.

One of the nature-of-the-beast characteristics of artistic endeavor is that it attracts attention—followers, fans, subscribers, students, likes, dislikes, critics, applause, reviews, comments, tweets, etc. The natural outgrowth of producing Transformational Creation and becoming a Transformational Creator is that it will draw people to you and to your work. Like it or not, you have placed yourself in a position of leadership. As you come out of isolation and mediocrity, fame, recognition, popularity, praise, disapproval, complaints, and criticism all come your way.

Although you might not be comfortable with these things, it's important to develop a healthy mindset about them so that you can use your influence for good. Today I hope to offer some guiding principles as we explore a few of these ideas together.

Fame, Popularity, and Influence

What is the distinction between influence, popularity, and fame? Why does it matter?

There are probably many layers of answers, but here is some food for thought:

> *Influence (noun): An emanation of spiritual or moral force; the act or power of producing an effect without apparent exertion of force or direct exercise of command; the power or capacity of causing an effect in indirect or intangible ways.*[1]
>
> *Influence (verb): To affect or alter by indirect or intangible means; to have an effect on the condition or development of.*[2]
>
> *Fame: Public estimation; popular acclaim; see also reputation, renown.*[3]
>
> *Famous: widely known; honored for achievement.*[4]
>
> *Popular: Of or relating to the general public; suitable to the majority; adapted to or indicative of the understanding and taste of the majority; suited to the means of the majority; frequently encountered or widely accepted; commonly liked or approved.*[5]

Fame means people know who you are. Popularity means people like who you are. Influence means people are affected by who you are and what you create.

These definitions raise even more questions. Is it necessary to have fame in order to have influence? Does fame always mean popularity? Does popularity mean influence? Does fame help or hinder our ability to influence? What do these definitions and the answers to these questions mean for your path?

Influence Is the Constant

Whatever you might answer to these questions, I would encourage you to examine your motives and the end that path will lead to. It's up to you to decide what kind of influence you will have. Of these three things—fame, popularity and influence—influence is the only thing that is constant. President Thomas S. Monson shared this principle in the following story:

> *More than 40 years ago, when President David O. McKay extended to me a call to the Quorum of the Twelve Apostles, he warmly welcomed me with a heartfelt smile and a tender embrace. Among the sacred counsel he extended was the declaration, "There is one responsibility that no one can evade. That is the effect of one's personal influence."*[6]

Synonyms for influence are *power, effect, leadership, impact.*[7] There is a pilot program currently underway at a regional university in the central United States that has as one of its purposes to prove that everything an individual thinks, says, does or feels affects others around them.[8] It aims to demonstrate that leadership is taking place whether or not one decides to engage in it.

There are many other studies that prove similar things. President Hinckley said that, as members of the Church, we are automatically placed in a position of leadership, the consequences of which "we cannot shrink nor run away [from] and which we must face up to with boldness and courage and ability."[9]

My point is that, as Artist-Disciples, we are leaders and we have influence, even if we're not famous or popular. Popularity might be the key for your mission, but not for others' missions. Fame might be necessary for your offering, but not for others' offerings. I just read through the *TIME 100 Most Influential People In the World* list for 2012. There were a lot of people on that list who were famous, and some who were not. There were a lot of people who were popular, and some who were not. There were some that were popular and famous, as well as influential, and some who were not. In all cases, though, these people were exercising influence.

How many likes...?

Ultimately, if we're trying to become like Jesus Christ—the most influential Being in the universe—then we are going to become influential. How many likes and dislikes would Jesus get today? He wasn't always popular, but He was famous and He had a lot of influence. I don't think Jesus set out for fame, but it came because of His influence. Influence, leadership, your personal power, the impact or effect you have—these are things you cannot run away from, and they are both a test and gift to help you and others transform to become like the Savior.

Keeping It in Perspective

So, as Artist-Disciples, we know we are going to have influence. That is a given. We also know that (depending on our mission/offering) we might have fame or popularity. So how do you deal with this kind of power and attention? I would like to share a few principles I have found about how to handle the attention of various forms you will attract as an Artist-Disciple so that your long-term influence is based around the Savior.

1. The Missionary Tag Approach

As natural followers come into our lives, what do we do with them?

I remember when I was in the Missionary Training Center in Provo, UT. One of the first lessons we received went something like this: "Elders and Sisters. What is the most important name on your name tag? Is it the name of the Church? Is it the title of Elder or Sister? Is it your last name?" Of course, you know the answer. The most important name on a full-time missionary's name tag is "Jesus Christ."

Later on in my mission I learned the importance of this principle. I was in my first area for 7½ months. During that time we taught many lessons and developed a pretty substantial teaching pool—over twenty investigators. When I left the area, I hoped they'd keep on taking the lessons. A month or so later I saw my former companion at a mission conference and asked him how things were going. He said that things were not going so well. Since I had left, about 16-17 of those investigators had stopped meeting with the missionaries. I was stunned. He said that they were all "too attached to Elder Brett, and not attached enough to the Lord." That experience taught me a valuable lesson. From that moment on I strove to attach people to the Savior, not to myself.

Since we are artists, people will naturally become attached to us and our personalities. That's part of the deal. What sets Artist-*Disciples* apart from artist *self-servers* or even simply artist *individuals* is our mentality and approach. Nephi taught that priestcraft is a state in which "men preach and set themselves up for a light unto the world, that they may get gain and praise of the world; but they seek not the welfare of Zion"[10]. This is obviously not a worthy approach for an Artist-Disciple.

We should seek to set Christ up as the light and ultimately lead those in our sphere of influence incrementally to Him. All of our systems, structures and interactions should reflect this mentality. To Artist-Disciples, a fan base is a flock—and we are shepherds, not sheepherders. We are shepherds leading the flock which we've been entrusted with back to the Good Shepherd.

2. Tyre and Hiram

On a different but related topic, a wise friend once shared this insight about the process of building the Temple of Solomon. David and Solomon, both priesthood leaders, led the project of building the temple, having received instructions from the Lord. But they did not do all the work themselves, nor did they confine themselves to only work with those who held the priesthood or were in the covenant. David collected a number of skilled workmen who had the ability to execute the temple plans and later, Solomon hired out the work in gold and brass from Tyre, specifically calling upon Hiram of the tribe of Naphtali.

The principle? As our sphere of influence expands, we will be naturally led to people of skill and influence who are not members of the Church. As mentioned in Lesson 1, Orson F. Whitney said that "God is using more than one people" to accomplish His work.[11] Many of these people will be like-minded. They are part of our sphere of influence, too, and they will help us produce Transformational Creation. We need to remember that there are millions and millions of good people throughout the earth that we can work with and have influence on. They may or may not join the Church in mortality, but whatever they decide to do, we must make sure we perform well with them too.

3. Adulation is Poison

Speaking to the men of the Church during a priesthood session of General Conference, President Dieter F. Uchtdorf shared the following experience:

> *When I was called as a General Authority, I was blessed to be tutored by many of the senior Brethren in the Church. One day I had the opportunity to drive President James E. Faust to a stake conference. During the hours we spent in the car, President Faust took the time to teach me some important principles about my assignment. He explained also how gracious the members of the Church are, especially to General Authorities. He said, "They will treat you very kindly. They will say nice things about you." He laughed a little and then said, "Dieter, be thankful for this. But don't you ever inhale it."*[12]

As we produce Transformational Creation and become more and more excellent at what we do, it is likely that we will also receive more and more praise and adulation. It is important to learn how to accept, not deflect, praise, and to do it humbly. The danger comes when we inhale.

A wise musician once told me that the best artists keep on improving because, "...they never feel like they've arrived." When we feel like we've arrived, that is precisely when our improvement starts to depart. Pride makes us feel like we have done it all ourselves, that we can do it all ourselves, and that we will do it all ourselves. James Phillips, a wise Church leader and friend, wrote the following:

> *...you must remember that adulation is poison. It happens to many, many successful and famous people. Before their fall they think that they did it; that they reached their success mostly on their own power. Their ego takes over and gets in the way. Then, they fall. One way to help with this inclination of our natural selves is with **every new day to think, say, and do something that humbles you to the core**. Try to do this humbling thing in the service of others. Another suggestion is to be grateful for any good things that you have in your life.*[13]

Another tendency of artists is to be hyper-critical of other artists and hyper-commendatory of ourselves. I love this counsel from the Prophet Joseph: "...Don't be limited in your views with regard to your neighbor's virtue, but beware of self-righteousness, and be limited in the estimate of your own virtues, and not think yourselves more righteous than others."[14]

Too often being critical of others reflects a selfish need for attention. We should remember Elder Maxwell's counsel, that "...those who 'shine as lights in the world' have no need to seek the spotlight!"[15] Pride is indeed the "universal sin"[16] and it can be especially ensnaring for Artist-Disciples. I've found power in acknowledging the Lord's hand in all things[17]. I've also found power to overcome pride in trying to be meek, humble, and lowly in heart. As you and I stay focused on our Three Rings and on exercising righteous influence, we develop the faith to "…be true in the dark and humble in the spotlight."[18]

Your Expanding Sphere of Influence

As we do all of these things we've talked about in this book and perform well within each of our Three Rings, our influence and power will grow. This is a natural outgrowth of becoming more like the Savior. President Kimball said it this way:

> *Each of us has more opportunities to do good and to be good than we ever use. These opportunities lie all around us. Whatever the size of our present circle of effective influence,* ***if we were to improve our performance even a little bit, that circle would be enlarged.*** *There are many individuals waiting to be touched and loved if we care enough to improve in our performance.*

What can you do to improve your performance, even a little bit? After all, it is for the service of God and His children that you do what you do. President Kimball continues this way:

> *We must remember that those mortals we meet in parking lots, offices, elevators, and elsewhere are that portion of mankind God has given us to love and to serve. It will do us little good to speak of the general brotherhood of mankind if we cannot regard those who are all around us as our brothers and sisters. If our sample of humanity seems unglamorous or so very small, we need to remember the parable Jesus gave us in which he reminded us that greatness is not always a matter of size or scale, but of the quality of one's life. If we do well with our talents and with the opportunities around us, this will not go unnoticed by God. And to those who do well with the opportunities given them, even more will be given!*[19]

Does it matter what size your plot is?

Our mission might be to 30, to 30,000, or to 30,000,000. Whatever the case, we need to perform well with that sample of humanity the Lord has trusted us with in order for it to grow. President Monson spoke to this principle by sharing the following poem:

> *"Father, where shall I work today?"*
> *And my love flowed warm and free.*
> *Then he pointed out a tiny spot*
> *And said, "Tend that for me."*
> *I answered quickly, "Oh no, not that!*
> *Why, no one would ever see,*
> *No matter how well my work was done.*
> *Not that little place for me."*
> *And the word he spoke, it was not stern; ...*
> *"Art thou working for them or for me?*
> *Nazareth was a little place,*
> *And so was Galilee."*[20]

Certainly we wouldn't judge the worth of Jesus' ministry by the size of his "plot," the distance of His travels, or the number of people He ministered to. Yet what great influence He had. Like President Kimball said, as we tend our plot well, the Lord will trust us and expand our sphere of influence. Our plot will grow. President Henry B. Eyring said, "The Lord sends prepared people to His prepared servants."[21] As we prepare ourselves, the Lord will send people ready to be influenced by us and our creative work.

This continual process of gaining excellence and transformation leads to natural followers, people who will support us so that we can keep doing what we are doing for a living. Spiritually-speaking, they are part of that sample of humanity the Lord has trusted us with. We must treat our fans and followers with love and respect and seek to bring them along the eternal progression continuum. As we seek to serve them, the influence we have can be lasting.

Country singer Bonnie Raitt said, "I think my fans will follow me into our combined old age. Real musicians and real fans stay together for a long, long time."[22] If we want fans, then we should focus on improving in our Three Rings and performing well with those we have.

Eternal Fans

So far it seems like we've only discussed our public influence, but all of these principles apply to our private influence as well. Those in our immediate stewardship—our families, those we serve in callings, friends, etc.—are ultimately our most important "fans".

If you were to ask me how to effectively minister to the masses, I would respond by saying that the best way to minister to the masses is to focus on "the one." Real change is accomplished one person or one family at a time. Our relationships with those in our public or professional influence will lead to those experiences with "the one," but most often it will be our relationships with those in our private influence that will lead to a special celestial rendezvous where true conversion is experienced.

Much of our work with "the masses" will be through the actual products we create. That's why it's important to try to create transformationally—so that our creations will touch them or connect with them in a way that leads them further along the eternal progression continuum, even if they just picked up our CD from iTunes, read our blog or watched one of our YouTube videos.

As we perform and create for the masses, we must not forget "the one" that hangs around after the show or e-mails us out of the blue because of how our work touched them. These are people with whom the Lord is trusting us. We must especially not forget the "one" and "ones" in our own families. We cannot let them down. In all that we do, we must remember that our influence is intended to bring people to Christ.

Arise and Shine Forth

I once had a conversation with a brilliant and capable returned missionary who happened to be a bit shy and introverted. The subject turned to how we enjoyed our individual mission experiences. I was shocked when he said, "I hated my mission." He went on to explain that he felt that the Church should not require shy or introverted missionaries to be outgoing, to knock doors, open their mouths, or put themselves "out there" to share the gospel. He felt like there were other things he would have been better suited for.

Can you relate? I had butterflies every day of my mission as I lifted my hand to knock the first door. But how is the gospel to be preached unless we put ourselves "out there"?

The Lord has commanded us to "…open [our] mouths and spare not," and He has promised, "Yea, open your mouths and they shall be filled."[23] Even if our creative work has nothing to do with our vocal cords, our "voice of life" will be filled as we open it and spare not. Whatever our creative work, we have to put ourselves "out there."

There was a faithful and dedicated sister missionary in my mission who said these inspiring words during her final testimony: "During my mission, nothing great ever happened inside my comfort zone."

The same thing can be said of our individual "missions" and creative offerings to God for the service of the world. Coming out of isolation and embracing influence will stretch us at times. But that is how all the great stuff happens. So we must not hold back. The Lord will strengthen us. Our influence is bound to grow as we stay in our Three Rings and get out of our comfort zones.

Questions and Action Items:

1. In your own words, what is the difference between fame, popularity, and influence? Which one do you want most for your artistic endeavors? Which one do you spend the most time on?

2. As in our discussion of Tyre and Hiram, is there someone outside your immediate circle who would be able to help you in your efforts to reach the people you are meant to reach? Create a list, and, as appropriate, ask for that help.

3. When was the last time you took time for "the one"? What effect did this have on you, and them?

Chapter Summary

- You cannot escape the responsibility or effect of your personal influence. Becoming a Transformational Creator and producing works of Transformational Creation places you in a position of leadership and influence.
- Fame means people know who you are. Popularity means people like who you are. Influence means people are affected by who you are and what you create. Every Artist-Disciple's mission involves influence but might not necessarily involve fame or popularity.
- In all of your shepherding and influencing make sure you are connecting your flock to Christ.
- Adulation is poison. Don't inhale it. Remain humble in the midst of recognition and expanding influence.
- Your sphere of influence will expand or contract in direct proportion to your performance with the sample of humanity you've been trusted with.

- In all your striving for fans make sure to remember the most important fans to love and influence: your family and the "one."

---

[1] Merriam-Webster Online Dictionary, merriam-webster.com/dictionary/influence.
[2] Merriam-Webster Online Dictionary, merriam-webster.com/dictionary/influence.
[3] Merriam-Webster Online Dictionary, merriam-webster.com/dictionary/fame.
[4] Merriam-Webster Online Dictionary, merriam-webster.com/dictionary/famous.
[5] Merriam-Webster Online Dictionary, merriam-webster.com/dictionary/popular.
[6] Thomas S. Monson, "Your Personal Influence," *Ensign,* May 2004.
[7] Merriam-Webster Online Dictionary, merriam-webster.com/thesaurus/influence.
[8] James I. Phillips, *Self-Leadership Change Project (SLCP).*
[9] Gordon B. Hinckley, "The Loneliness of Leadership," Brigham Young University Speeches of the Year. November 4, 1969.
[10] 2 Nephi 26:29.
[11] Orson F. Whitney, "Too Vast, Too Arduous, For Any One People," in Conference Report, April 1928, 59.
[12] Dieter F. Uchtdorf, "Pride and the Priesthood," *Ensign,* November 2010.
[13] Phillips, *Self-Leadership Change Project (SLCP),* emphasis added.
[14] Joseph Smith, as quoted by The Church of Jesus Christ of Latter-day Saints, *Teachings of Presidents of the Church: Joseph Smith,* ch. 37.
[15] Neal A. Maxwell, "In Him All Things Hold Together," BYU Devotional, March 31, 1991.
[16] Ezra Taft Benson, "Beware of Pride," *Ensign,* May 1989.
[17] Doctrine and Covenants 59:21.
[18] Jon M. Huntsman, "God Did Not Send Us Here to Fail," BYU Devotional, November 10, 2009.
[19] Spencer W. Kimball, "Jesus: The Perfect Leader," *Ensign,* August 1979, emphasis added .
[20] Meade MacGuire, as quoted by Thomas S. Monson, "Your Personal Influence," *Ensign,* May 2004.
[21] Henry B. Eyring, "A Child and a Disciple," *Ensign,* April 2003.
[22] Bonnie Raitt, as quoted by David Baskerville, *Music Business Handbook and Career Guide,* 243.
[23] Doctrine and Covenants 33:9-10.

Lesson 12:
Your Legacy

Artist-Disciple Insights

Mary's Story: Leaving a Legacy

"There is beauty all around, when there's Love at Home…"

I can remember it like it was yesterday, instead of many yesterdays ago. My dad's arm was around me. In fact, his arms were around all 8 of us, 7 children and my mother. I can still feel those arms now. I can remember the room, the stage, the building, everything. It was a ward talent show and our family was singing together, and my dad's long arms were around all of us.

Somehow the words of the hymn took on new meaning. Amid the daily challenges—and there were many—I knew that because we had love at home, because my parents loved me, the whole world could be beautiful.

My dad grew up singing with a mother who played the organ for church. Dad had a beautiful bass voice, but his greatest power was the love he put into it. When he sang, all the challenges and sorrows of life would disappear. I loved hearing him sing. I could feel his love for me, God's love for me, and it made me love them both more. It was my first recognition of what the Spirit feels like.

Mother was a different matter. She had a musical family, but somehow the talent seemed to miss her. She loved to sing but could not carry a tune. It was so bad that, as a child, her sisters would put their hands over their ears and plead with her to "Stop!" But she didn't stop. She kept singing.

Someone has said that music is the language of the heart. I would say that if I have any heart, it is because of the music I experienced as a child. My parents didn't have much—not in worldly possessions. They were raising children, not riches. But they did give us piano lessons. And we sang in the ward choir.

Those hours of singing together as a family have influenced me in countless ways. Some are easy to see, others more subtle. I look at obstacles differently because of my mother's willingness to keep singing. I learned togetherness in a family, helping one another, admiration for the way my parents dealt with their own challenges. So many things.

By the time I was a mother with several children of my own, [Mother] was considered one of the strong altos in the choir. Now we sing as a family, and the ripples keep going. When I direct the ward choir, I encourage "non-singers" to come and share their testimony with us. Lives continue to be changed through music.

What a legacy my parents left me.

The Finale

Congratulations!

You've made it this far. How have you progressed as an Artist-Disciple?

Can you see how important you are not only as an artist and creator, but also as a disciple and a leader? Do you have a greater understanding of your place and purpose at this time? Are you ready to do your part in fulfilling prophetic vision and preparing the earth for the most glorious time yet?

I hope you realize more than ever that you are not alone. As Artist-Disciples, we are part of something greater than ourselves, and we *can* impact the laws, culture, and lives of those around us. Have you written down the impressions *you* are receiving?

As we wrap up our time together, I'd like to share a few encouraging words about success in the Lord's way.

What Is Success?

I once received an e-mail from a fellow Artist-Disciple serving as a full-time missionary in the field. He wrote:

> *Does the feeling of anxiety stop? I'm seriously really happy and learning more than ever. I do feel sometimes though like my heart just is going way fast and that if I'm not doing something then I'm sinning or something like that...I don't really know how to explain it, and I want to overcome it. Maybe it's [because I'm] not giving myself any slack. Sometimes I think I demand perfection from myself while not letting myself realize that I'm not perfect...*

Does this sound familiar? As an Artist-Disciple, there are questions that you and I will inevitably face, such as "What is success?" "When are my efforts 'enough'?" Unfortunately, many of us as Latter-day Saints struggle to "do all we can do,"[1] but we never know when we've done all that can be done. We can often or constantly feel guilty, insufficient, even unworthy.

Perhaps in part because of our desire to create and beautify the world around us, artists are also often some of the most insecure and perfectionistic people I know. This amplifies the problem. We always feel like we could have done better, or we compare our work to other artists' work and we don't feel like we measure up. We hope people will "like" what we've done and criticism knocks our house of cards to the ground. There always seems to be a wide gap between our ambition and our ability.

For pure peace of mind, it's helpful to remember that true success is spiritually rooted. As you strive for excellence as an Artist-Disciple, your own insight into the definition of success will be increasingly important. I hope the following thoughts will assist you towards that end.

Christocentric Success

> *My main purpose and goal in performing is to uplift, enlighten, and invite to come unto Christ.* – TAD member Paul

As an artist, how do you know you've been "successful"? Just as there are many false "idols" we can center our lives on, as we discussed in Lesson 5, so there are many other ways we can measure success that are more or less damaging. Business coach Daniel Midson-Short identified six different types of success:

1. **Puritan.** *Work as hard as possible to prove yourself as "worthy."…Each achievement adds more to [your] sense of worthiness, and there is always another goal once the current one is achieved.*
2. **Materialistic.** *Gain as much luxury and status as possible…Media and society seems to promote and almost worship those individuals who have a great deal of money or possessions.*
3. **Power.** *Gain as much control as possible. Similar to the material view, the power view wants to control and be the person who chooses.*
4. **Spiritual.** *Detach from "temptations" in life and transcend the present…choose to resist desires for material gratification, instead choosing to be connected to rewards in the spiritual realm.*
5. **Contributor.** *Create a better world for other people and future generations…It doesn't have to be on a world scale, it can simply be the desire to help people through their everyday struggles.*
6. **Escapist.** *Have as much fun and as many peak experiences as possible. These people believe life is simply one big experience. Our time on earth is meant to be lived to the fullest and we are meant to "live deep and suck out all the marrow of life," as Henry David Thoreau famously espoused.*[2]

What is your measure of success? In which of these areas do you spend the most time?

As much as we'd like to say that we always get our sense of success from the "spiritual," it's probably true that we don't. At different times and seasons in life—even at different times during a given day—we experience "success" in any of these six strata or other centers. And that is probably okay, as long as we are clear about what our ultimate center really is. For example, it's okay to feel joy and satisfaction because of a monetary success but if this becomes our permanent or long-term center, then we are in trouble.

For Artist-Disciples, the ultimate measurement of success is what I call Christocentric Success. It is a companion to Christocentric Creation. As with all things, Christ is the only center or measure that makes *everything* clear, that brings everything into focus. We could focus on family or work, and many things around us would become clearer while others would get more blurry. If we focus on fame and recognition, then we might achieve success in that area, but perhaps to the neglect of family or Church. If we focus on Christ, though, then everything comes into focus.

Measuring all our success based on His principles opens us to success in money, family, Church *and* all the other centers and strata. He is the only center that makes all things possible.[3] If our "desired outcome" is to become like Christ and He is our center, then we can achieve anything. This is Christocentric Success, and as Artist-Disciples, it can catapult us into joys and experiences we never knew existed.

Transformational Success

> *I am now more motivated to do things to bring joy to others than to do them for myself. I find satisfaction in working hard toward something, whether it's as simple as calming a crying child or*

choreographing four bars of eight, and doing it well enough that it blesses the lives of others. – TAD member Briahna

Just like Christocentric Creation had as one of its characteristics Transformational Creation, so too does Christocentric Success have as one of its characteristics Transformational Success.

When it comes to your creative work, how do you define your victories? Is it how big your audience is? Is it how much people like or approve of your work? Is it numbers of sales? These may be components of your success formula depending on the type of work you do, but none of them should be the ultimate aim of your work.

Transformational Success is based on this principle which Elder Dallin H. Oaks taught gospel teachers in 1999. Substitute your particular creative work in place of references Elder Oaks makes to teaching or teachers:

> *A gospel teacher is concerned with the results of his or her teaching, and such a teacher will measure the success of teaching and testifying by its <u>impact on the lives of the learners</u>. A gospel teacher will never be satisfied with just delivering a message or preaching a sermon. A superior gospel teacher wants to assist in the Lord's work to bring eternal life to His children.*[4]

Transformational Creation seeks to transform people. Transformational Success is its corollary, which defines success in creation based on how your creation affects and builds others, the Kingdom, and yourself.

Did you give all that you have?

These results may be visible and immediate, or they may come years down the road, but the true Artist-Disciple seeks to assist in the Lord's work by seeking to transform people, and finds his or her success in that *effort*. This does not mean that we are a failure if our entire audience does not get baptized. Because people have agency, Transformational Success is measured primarily by *our* commitment, desire and effort to transform people. It really is a matter of the heart.

I also love these lines from *Preach My Gospel*: "When you have done your very best, you may still experience disappointments, but you will not be disappointed in yourself. You can feel certain that the Lord is pleased when you feel the Spirit working through you."[5] This rings true for me since Transformational Success seeks results in people's lives and those results are impossible without the Spirit.

Lift Where You Stand

> *I decided to make the goal of performing...in church...And after about 3 months I reached my goal! ...For the first time in my life I now enjoy playing the piano! My whole life I've hated practicing...But now playing the piano has become a joy, it is something I can't get enough of and has become a great stress-reliever in my life. In conclusion, the overarching truth I have learned from this journey is...dreams will one day be reality, given enough time and work in the Lord's service! – TAD member Paul*

Whether you are preparing for a major concert or a sacrament meeting performance, you might be concerned about the size of your success or that your talents are insignificant and won't make a contribution to the world. Henry Van Dyke wrote, "Use the talents you possess, for the woods would be very silent if no birds sang except the best."[6]

LDS musician Richard Parkinson said that he believes that,

> *We all carry responsibilities through the talents that we have been given to take care of each other, lift each other and make each other feel good. Some talents are more on display than others and sometimes I wish it wasn't that way because it's the small, what*

we would consider "insignificant" talents that really make the world go around.[7]

No matter the size of your sphere of influence or the visibility of your talents, your contribution is absolutely crucial to the unfolding work of the Kingdom of God. I hope you believe this.

President Uchtdorf's Story

Consider the principle taught in the following story, shared by President Dieter F. Uchtdorf in the October 2008 General Conference Priesthood session:

> *Some years ago...a group of brethren was asked to move a grand piano from the chapel to the adjoining cultural hall, where it was needed for a musical event. None were professional movers, and the task of getting that gravity-friendly instrument through the chapel and into the cultural hall seemed nearly impossible....As they stood around the piano, uncertain of what to do next, a good friend of mine...spoke up. He said, "Brethren, stand close together and lift where you stand."*
>
> *It seemed too simple. Nevertheless, each lifted where he stood, and the piano rose from the ground and moved into the cultural hall as if on its own power...*[8]

What is it we are trying to lift as Artist-Disciples? The culture, morals, faith, and happiness of the world. We seek to bring others to Christ, and the only way we can do so is if each one of us "lifts where we stand."

The Apostle Paul taught that we are all one, united in the body of Christ, and that, although each of us might play a different part, there is no part more important than the others. Actually he said that if any parts are more important than others, it is the less visible parts.

He said, "…those members of the body, which seem to be more feeble, are necessary."[9]

In the end, it's not about individuals, it's about a team. As President Uchtdorf said "none of us can or should move the Lord's work alone. But if we all stand close together in the place the Lord has appointed and lift where we stand, nothing can keep this divine work from moving upward and forward."[10]

What is it that you have to share? What is your contribution? Remember Stephen Pressfield's words: "Creative work is…a gift to the world and every being in it. Don't cheat us of your contribution. Give us what you've got"[11]

Perfection and Practice

> *I like the way I feel when I engage in my creative work. I feel as if it is a way to thank my Heavenly Father for the gifts and talents he has given me by "living up to my privileges." I also like that it is a part of me. Part of Kendra…is her music and her voice. So it would seem that when I create art I am also creating myself. To be honest, I just plain old like making the music... –* TAD Member Kendra

Remember our Artist-Disciple friend who wrote me about his desire to be perfect? I think most Artist-Disciples have dealt with a similar feeling. This is part of what I replied to him:

You have two options as I see it –

1. *Give up and give in to the natural man by becoming lazy and cutting yourself too much slack. This would be an abuse; or*
2. *Learn to overcome the anxiety and arrive at power and peace in your life through the grace of Christ. This will require that you learn more about grace and cut yourself slack in the Lord's way.*

For me, power, peace and a feeling of success have been found as I've learned to understand and be okay with the fact that perfection is not required of us in mortality. I've learned that the grace of Christ is sufficient to make up for my mortal weaknesses and He is helping me every step of the way.

The Finisher's Touch

Brother Brad Wilcox, a Church Educational System instructor and author of several books, explains the process that we must all go through of learning to rely on the Lord's grace by comparing Christ's arrangement with us to a mom providing piano lessons for her child. The mom pays the debt in full and then can ask something of the child—practice. In this life, we are *practicing* to become like the Savior.

> *When learning the piano, are the only options performing at Carnegie Hall or quitting? No. Growth and development take time. Learning takes time. When we understand grace, we understand that God is long-suffering, that change is a process, and that repentance is a pattern in our lives…So grace is not a booster engine that kicks in once our fuel supply is exhausted. Rather, it is our constant energy source. It is not the light at the end of the tunnel but the light that moves us through the tunnel. Grace is not achieved somewhere down the road. It is received right here and right now. It is not a finishing touch; it is the Finisher's touch. (see Hebrews 12:2)*[12]

Ultimately, all of our success comes back to the One through whom success is possible, whether we are teaching a class, composing a symphony, or concocting a dinner. Our success is given and measured through the grace of Christ.

Your Best and the Lord's Best

> *The gospel of Jesus Christ plays an originating, inspirational, directional, encouraging, goal-setting, joyful, every-breath-I-take role in my creative work. And more.* – TAD member Debbie

During my final testimony as a full-time missionary I felt the confirmation of the Spirit that I had been successful. I was then inspired to say these words,

> *I have done my best. I have not done the best, but I have done my best. Would I go back and do some things differently with the knowledge I now have? Absolutely. But at the time, I was doing the best I could with the knowledge I then had. I have done my best.*

In all thoughts on success, there remains the underlying interplay between doing all that you can do and relying on the Lord's grace. This definition accords with how John Wooden described success: "Success is peace of mind which is a direct result of self-satisfaction in knowing you did your best to become the best you are capable of becoming."[13]

Always do *your* best in all three of your Rings and trust the Lord to do *His* best to assist you in every step of the process. As you focus your idea of success in Christ and His grace, in transforming people and in doing your best, you will be able to look back at your day, your life and your creative work and say "…it [is] good."[14]

Legacy: What will your legacy be?

> *One goal that I have had for a long time is to create a network of theaters and media to give Artist-Disciples a vehicle and venue to create the art that will transform themselves and their audience, and also be a safe environment where artists not only don't have to compromise their values but are encouraged to have high*

> *values, a place where education can continue and families can be supported. I think that something like that would give artists a greater opportunity to change the world of entertainment and media more directly.* – TAD member Jason

The inspiration for discussing legacy in this course came to me as I listened to an interview with LDS comedian Keith Stubbs. In it he said that he wanted to do "stuff" that his children could watch. He didn't want to leave anything behind that his children couldn't watch. His goal was to leave a legacy of good clean comedy.[15]

What are you going to leave behind? What do you desire to be known for? What do you want to create for your children, your grandchildren, the Church, and the rest of the world?

This quotation from President Harold B. Lee about gospel teachers can serve as our template as we consider the topic of legacy. I've revised it for our purposes:

> *The calling of [the Artist-Disciple] is one of the noblest in the world. The good [Artist-Disciple] can make all the difference in inspiring boys and girls and men and women to change their lives and fulfill their highest destiny. The importance of [the Artist-Disciple] has been beautifully described by Daniel Webster when he said, "If we work upon marble, it will perish; if we work upon brass, time will efface it; but if we work upon immortal minds, if we imbue them with principles and the just fear of God and love of our fellowman, we engrave upon those tablets something that will brighten through all eternity."*[16]

United States President Woodrow Wilson spoke about our purpose in life and said, "You are not here merely to make a living. You are here to enable the world to live more amply, with greater vision, and with a finer spirit of hope and achievement. You are here to enrich the world. You impoverish yourself if you forget this errand."[17]

As stewards of this earth, we have a responsibility to leave it better than we found it. We also need to realize that we are the rich inheritors of the legacies of so many giants who have gone before us, and that we can build more structures for future generations to build on, as well. Amelia Earhart said, "Some of us have great runways already built for us. If you have one, take off! But if you don't have one, realize it is your responsibility to grab a shovel and build one for yourself and for those who will follow after you."[18]

Karlyn's Story

I have had "great runways" built by those who have gone before me. The following story is from a TAD participant who also happens to be my grandmother, Karlyn:

> *In November of 1980 the Bellevue, WA. L.D.S. Temple was dedicated by Pres. Spencer W. Kimball. I was privileged to conduct one of the choirs that sang at the dedication services...The members had worked long and hard for many months, sacrificing time and money in order to attend rehearsals, and had worked diligently on perfecting their voices for this momentous occasion.*
>
> *On the morning that our choir sang, we were warming up in the Celestial room—all dressed in white robes, and eager to please our Father and Savior...hearts were full, and voices eager. As they raised their voices at my signal to bring them in on the first chord of just our warm up, at our sound all of our eyes moved instantly heavenward as we could literally hear heavenly choirs join us. It was as though there was NO ceiling at that moment in the Temple— just a conduit straight from Heaven to us, and us to them. It was a mesmerizing, exceedingly inspiring moment...one never to be forgotten.*
>
> *A few minutes later, I was standing just a couple of feet directly in front of our dear Prophet, Spencer W. Kimball, directing this*

same chosen choir in "The Lord's Prayer," "Bless this House"—and of course, "The Spirit of God" with the "Hallelujah Shout." What a blessed experience that was, for which I will be ever grateful.

Part of leaving a legacy is leaving a record. I am so grateful my grandmother and other ancestors have left behind records of their experiences. It has helped me to build on their legacies. As author and friend Randal Wright wrote, "Imagine an Einstein, Newton, or Edison taking what they discovered to the grave!"[19] Recording what we discover and learn is one of the best ways to leave a legacy, for the world and especially for our children.

Forget Yourself into Immortality

Ultimately, a spiritual legacy is the best kind of legacy to leave behind. There are many important priorities in life, but our most meaningful legacy will be left as we prioritize the spiritual in all three of our Rings. The great Greek statesman Pericles reportedly said, "What you leave behind is not what is engraved in stone monuments, but what is woven into the lives of others."[20] When it comes to our creative work, as we've discussed in virtually everything throughout this course, we should seek to invest our legacy in the transformation of people—a Transformational Legacy.

That being said, we need not worry too much about leaving a legacy. Ultimately, a legacy is not left so much as it is lived. Once we've examined the righteous ends we seek, we can then safely lay them aside and focus on serving people. How does this summary statement attributed to the poet Ralph Waldo Emerson apply to you?

> *The mass of men worry themselves into nameless graves while here and there a great unselfish soul forgets himself into immortality.*[21]

Conclusion: Remember Lot's Wife

> *Yes, I love performing, but it's not necessarily all "lights and glamour"...as you know. It's hard work, takes a ton of dedication and persistence. Sometimes I wish I could just go home and be "normal." But then I remind myself that normal is relative and, if I were to find myself in a "normal" situation, I would most likely find myself wishing for a more adventurous life. The grass is always greener!* – TAD member Meghan

Author Joseph Campbell was famous for his statement, "Follow your bliss." Later, after more life experience, he wrote, "I should have said, follow your blisters."[22]

The Lord's work is not easy and just because we feel *inspired* by a mission does not mean every step will be blissful. When doubts, fears, depression, fatigue, criticisms, or other challenges come your way, don't turn back. Remember Lot's wife. Instead of imagining all the things that could go wrong, imagine all the things that the world would be missing if you turned back and gave up on your mission. What songs would the world never hear? What poems would they never be inspired by? What lives would not be touched and transformed?

He will give us success

I, like you, have experienced my fair share of frustrations and setbacks in my journey. I am inspired by the words of the Book of Mormon prophet Ammon, who described some of the trials he and the other sons of Mosiah went through on their missions and how the Lord helped them overcome. "Now when our hearts were depressed, and *we were about to turn back*, behold, the Lord comforted us, and said: Go amongst thy brethren, the Lamanites, and bear with patience thine afflictions, and *I will give unto you success.*"[23]

There is great success and joy to be had as we hang in there and rely on the Lord for strength. But if we turn back, we'll never experience it. LDS author Randal Wright taught about what we can learn from the sons of Mosiah's mission experience:

> *Because they went forward with faith, they felt the joy of victory...Because they stayed steadfast and sure, thousands were converted to the truth in their day, and now millions have been inspired by their story in our day. All too often we feel motivated to accomplish something of great importance, but we soon abandon the mission before it even begins. Or we turn back before it is completed and miss the joy that could have been ours.*[24]

The doing might be hard, but there is great joy to be experienced during and after our journey if we don't turn back. We need to have the resolve to fight resistance in all forms and say, as did Nehemiah, "I am doing a great work, so that I cannot come down."[25]

What's next?

Many blessings will come to you as you endure to the end in completing the different components of your mission in life. President Spencer W. Kimball said, "One of the rich rewards coming from doing great things is the capacity to do still greater things."[26]

There is always another blank canvas. There is always the next show. There is always another dream castle to build. As you stick to it, you will be more and more able to accomplish even greater things for the Lord. You will be able to give the same response that one great artist did when he was asked which of all his productions was the greatest. His prompt answer was, "The next."[27]

May we find excitement in the exertion, joy in the doing, and that special rest that comes after we cheerfully do all that is in our power and then stand still to see the arm of the Lord revealed. There will be hard times, but may we so live as to hear those precious words, "Well done, thou good and faithful servant..."[28] "Remember Lot's wife"[29] and don't look back or give up.

Graduation

What a journey we have been on together! You probably don't have robes or a cap on right now, but consider this your commencement ceremony. You are about to "commence" on an incredible adventure that has been introduced by the concepts in this book, but is only just beginning in your life. There are places to go and things to do.

By now you should understand the preeminent importance of discipleship in your life and in your creative work. In fact, as a symbolic way of remembering this principle, I invite you to figuratively turn the Artist-Disciple tassel and consider yourself not only an Artist-Disciple, but a Disciple-Artist as well. We might always refer to this book and to each other as Artist-Disciples because, frankly, it's catchier. But—as we graduate from this TAD experience together—I hope we'll never forget that disciple always comes before artist and God's work and glory is always our first and foremost reason for creating.

Your hour is coming

As Artist-Disciples, we have the power to change the world for good. It is part of our spiritual identity and heritage as members of the Church of Jesus Christ of Latter-day Saints. The prophet Joseph Smith taught about the power of the Saints in this way:

> *I see no faults in the Church, and therefore let me be resurrected with the Saints, whether I ascend to heaven or descend to hell, or go to any other place. And if we go to hell, we will turn the devils*

out of doors and make a heaven of it. Where this people are, there is good society.[30]

The world might be descending further and further into spiritual and moral decadence, but as Artist-Disciples with the Lord's power we can lift it up and make a heaven out of it. We can improve the glory of the earth by adopting the Lord's work and glory as our own and by preparing for the great era of opportunity that awaits us. You and I can and will do it, because it is our destiny.

Winston Churchill said:

> *To every man there comes…that special moment when he is figuratively tapped on the shoulder and offered a chance to do a special thing unique to him and fitted to his talent. What a tragedy if that moment finds him unprepared or unqualified for the work which would be his finest hour.*[31]

I promise that opportunities for us as Artist-Disciples are here and they are coming. You could be tapped on the shoulder sooner than you think.

Get ready.

Questions and Action Items:

1. What is your next step? As a Disciple-Artist, how are you going to step into your role as an artist and creator who is preparing the world for the Second Coming?

2. What kind of legacy has been left to you, artistically and in life? What are you going to leave for others?

3. Now that you've completed this book, what does it mean to you to be a disciple?

...And an invitation

The biggest challenges I see in Artist-Disciples (or Disciple-Artists) as they start out on their path are #1 *staying* inspired and #2 *knowing* what to do next as they follow-up with their decision to change the world through the arts. May I share with you one way I've created to help you get through these challenges?

Throughout this book you've heard me mention the TAD 101 classes, and you've read some of the experiences and stories from other incredible Artist-Disciples involved. TAD is a place for Artist-Disciples who want to make a difference through their creative work and connect with a global community dedicated to doing the same thing. Members of TAD courses and the TAD community are the vanguard in a movement that will soon encompass transformational artists from all denominations and backgrounds. Together we are working to transform the airwaves, homes, lives, and laws of our nations so that they reflect what is good and true.

If you've been inspired by this journey and the concepts we've discussed together, I invite you to enroll in a TAD 101 course and join our international online community. Check out www.theartistdisciple.com to get started. The movement toward a better world through the arts is just beginning. Isn't it time you were a part of it?

---

[1] 2 Nephi 25:23.
[2] Daniel Midson-Short, "Six Types of Success," health-wealth.co.nz/home/free-articles/six-types-of-success.html.
[3] Philippians 4:13.
[4] Dallin H. Oaks, "Gospel Teaching," *Ensign*, November 1999, emphasis added.
[5] The Church of Jesus Christ of Latter-day Saints, *Preach My Gospel*, 10-11.
[6] Henry Van Dyke, bookbrowse.com/quotes/detail/index.cfm?quote_number=224.
[7] Nicole Sheahan, "Inside Mormon Music: Inside the Life of a Songwriter," deseretnews.com/article/705377127/Inside-the-life-of-a-songwriter.html?pg=all
[8] Dieter F. Uchtdorf, "Lift Where You Stand," *Ensign*, November 2008.
[9] 1 Corinthians 12:22.

10. Uchtdorf, "Lift Where You Stand," *Ensign,* November 2008.
11. Stephen Pressfield, goodreads.com/quotes/4301-creative-work-is-not-a-selfish-act-or-a-bid.
12. Brad Wilcox, "His Grace Is Sufficient," BYU Devotional, July 12, 2012.
13. John Wooden, brainyquote.com/quotes/quotes/j/johnwooden402561.html
14. Genesis 1:25.
15. Keith Stubbs, "Discussion 27: Clean Comedy," Everything Creative Podcast.
16. Harold B. Lee, as quoted by Dallin H. Oaks, "Gospel Teaching," *Ensign,* November 1999.
17. Woodrow Wilson, as quoted by Joan Garrett, *The Journey Continues: Life's Travel Guide for Teens and Young Adults,* 166.
18. Amelia Earhart, goodreads.com/quotes/596624-some-of-us-have-great-runways-already-built-for-us.
19. Randal Wright, *Achieving Your Life Mission,* 191.
20. Pericles, brainyquote.com/quotes/quotes/p/pericles387387.html.
21. Ralph Waldo Emerson, inspirednationonline.com/1/post/2012/01/forget-yourself-into-immortality.html
22. Joseph Campbell, as quoted by Jeffery Thompson, "What Is Your Calling In Life?" BYU Devotional, June 1, 2010.
23. Alma 26:27, emphasis added.
24. Wright, *Achieving Your Life Mission,* 201, emphasis added.
25. Nehemiah 6:3.
26. Spencer W. Kimball, "Education for Eternity," BYU Annual Faculty Conference, September 12, 1967.
27. Kimball, "Education for Eternity," BYU Annual Faculty Conference, September 12, 1967.
28. Matthew 25:21.
29. Luke 17:32.
30. Joseph Smith, as quoted by The Church of Jesus Christ of Latter-day Saints, *Teachings of the Presidents of the Church: Joseph Smith,* 524.
31. Winston Churchill, as quoted by Jeffrey R. Holland, "Sanctify Yourselves," *Ensign,* November 2000.

Take your Artist-Discipleship to the next level with these exciting TAD offerings:

TAD 101 COURSE
The course that started it all. Go deeper with Brydon and other Artist-Disciples from around the world in a transformational 8-week experience. Next course: Fall 2013.

TAD RETREAT
Get energized with a special 2-3 day retreat in Branson, MO with Brydon and other Artist-Disciples. Workshop, experience great live entertainment, showcase your talents, and much more. Stay tuned for more information.

THE ARTIST-DISCIPLE WORKBOOK
Coming soon! A companion to *The Artist-Disciple* book, *The Artist-Disciple Workbook* will help you explore TAD principles more deeply with study activities, helpful resources and bonus content not included in the original book.

TAD AUDIO
Coming soon! Program yourself with winning principles and habits by listening to TAD Audio products at home, on the road or wherever you take your iPod.

Visit www.theartistdisciple.com to get started!

Made in the USA
San Bernardino, CA
20 December 2013